ESSENTIAL

DATE DUE

Corfu: Regions and Best places to see

Original text by Des Hannigan
Updated by Des Hannigan

© Automobile Association Developments Limited 2007
First published 2007

ISBN-10: 0-7495-4948-3
ISBN-13: 978-0-7495-4948-0

Published by AA Publishing, a trading name of Automobile Association Developments
Limited, whose registered office is Fanum House, Basing View, Basingstoke,
Hampshire RG21 4EA.
Registered number 1878835.

Colour separation: MRM Graphics Ltd
Printed and bound in Italy by Printer Trento S.r.l.

A02694
Maps in this title produced from mapping © Freytag-Berndt u. Artaria KG,
1231 Vienna-Austria

About this book

> **Symbols are used to denote the following categories:**
>
> ✚ map reference to maps on cover
> ✉ address or location
> ☎ telephone number
> 🕑 opening times
> ✋ admission charge
> 🍴 restaurant or café on premises
>   or nearby
> Ⓜ nearest underground train station
>
> 🚍 nearest bus/tram route
> 🚉 nearest overground train station
> 🚢 nearest ferry stop
> ✈ nearest airport
> ↔ other places of interest nearby
> ❓ other practical information
> ➤ indicates the page where you will
>   find a fuller description

This book is divided into five sections.

The essence of Corfu pages 6–19
Introduction; Features; Food and Drink;
Short Break including the 10 Essentials

Planning pages 20–33
Before You Go; Getting There; Getting
Around; Being There

Best places to see pages 34–55
The unmissable highlights of any visit
to Corfu

Best things to do pages 56–77
Excellent restaurants; activities;
museums, art galleries and exhibitions;
places to take the children; best beaches
and more

Exploring pages 78–187
The best places to visit in Corfu,
organized by area

Maps
All map references are to the maps on
the covers. For example, Kérkyra has the
reference ✚ 32S – indicating the grid
square in which it is to be found

Prices
An indication of the cost of restaurants
and cafés at attractions is given by
€ signs: €€€ denotes higher prices,
€€ denotes average prices, € denotes
lower prices

Hotel prices
Price are per room per night: € budget
(under €60); €€ moderate (€60–€100);
€€€ expensive to luxury (over €100)

Restaurant prices
Price for a three-course meal per person
without drinks: € budget (under €15);
€€ moderate (€15–€25); €€€ expensive
(over €25)

Contents

The essence of...

Corfu's glorious beaches, seductive food and buzzing nightlife is more than enough to keep you happy without you ever having to leave your favourite resort. But hidden Corfu, the astonishing variety of the island's countryside, the charm and colour of Venetian Corfu Town, the timeless appeal of country villages – none of these should be missed. Relax, soak up the sun, but plan adventures and set aside days for exploring, too. Sample as much as you can and take away a mix of happy memories.

features

Corfu can take your breath away with its natural beauty and its sundrenched light. It is still the 'Garden Isle' of Greece, although it may seem rather trampled in one or two resorts where conspicuous tourism has overwhelmed everyday life. It is an island that has been enriched by its dramatic past and it is still a place where you can live out your Greek island dreams. Corfu was always at the heart of Mediterranean events, a crossroads of East and West that has remained essentially Greek at heart, in spite of the impact of Byzantine, Roman and Venetian cultures and the later British and French influences.

Many things define the essence of Corfu. There is, of course, the exquisite heat of summer, the silken beaches and the crystal-clear sea. But Corfu is an all-year-round experience – the fragrance of orange blossom in winter; the brilliant colours of wild flowers in spring and autumn; the excitement

of a festival; the soft chimes of sheep bells in mountain meadows; the hissing of cicadas in the heat; and the musky scent of pine. Then there are the early mornings on the western beaches when the coolness of the night lingers on the sea air;

hushed afternoons in remote mountain villages; the sweetness of a summer's dusk after a long day of sea and sun; feasts of traditional Greek food and wine in village tavernas; sunset drinks above the glittering Mediterranean.

Above all, there are the people of the island – the Corfiots – who will always make visitors feel at home.

GEOGRAPHY
● Corfu is the most northerly of the Ionian Islands. The southeast coast lies about 10km (6 miles) from mainland Greece, the northeast about 2km (1 mile) from Albania. The length, north to south, is 60km (37 miles); and the width, east to west, is 4 to 30km (2.5 to 19 miles). The length of the coastline is 217km (134 miles).

CLIMATE
● The highest monthly rainfall is in December, with 240mm (9in). Summer months are mostly dry.
● The average daily sunshine from May to September is 10 hours.
● The average temperature, July to August, is 32°C (89°F); December to January, 15°C (59°F).

POPULATION
● The island has a population of approximately 114,000, of which about 41,000 live in Corfu Town.

HIGHEST POINT
● Mount Pandokrator, at 906m (2,971ft), is the highest point of the island.

ECONOMIC FACTORS
● About 65 per cent of Corfu's land is under cultivation. Of this, 55 per cent is devoted to olive trees, of which there are an estimated 3.5 million.

food & drink

Greek cooking has languished unfairly in the shadow of French and Italian cuisine. But the best Greek tavernas know the value of traditional cooking enhanced with international influences and today, eating out, especially on this cosmopolitan island, can be a rewarding experience.

MEZEDES

Mezedes, or *mezes* (starters), can be a feast by themselves and true *aficionados* may never get beyond them in a good taverna. *Mezes* are a communal experience to the Greeks. Everyone digs in. Try *keftedes* (spicy meat balls); *bourekakia* (meat pies); *kotópoulo* (chicken portions); *saligkaria* (snails); *manitaria* (mushrooms); *spanokeftedes* (spinach balls); *dolmadakia* (vine leaves stuffed with rice); *saganáki* (fried cheese); *horta* or *tsigarelli* (wild greens tossed in oil and lemon juice); and *elies* (olives). Throw in dips such as *tzatzíki* (yoghurt, garlic and cucumber), or *melitzanasalata* (aubergine and garlic), and drink wine in copious amounts…

MEAT DISHES

There is a tradition of casserole cooking on Corfu. Try *pastitsada*, a Corfu speciality with an Italian touch that derives from Venetian *spezzatino*. It is

created from layered pasta, meat or veal and tomato filling, with bechamel sauce, paprika, cinnamon, and cheese topping. True Corfiot *pastitsada* is made with cockerel. *Sofrito* is another Corfiot speciality. It should contain veal preferably, or beef, cooked in white sauce with olive oil, wine vinegar, garlic and onion, plus white pepper to encourage a thirst. For a good *souvlaki* (shish kebab) ask for lamb *(arnisio)*, the very best. Pork *(hirinos) souvlaki* is also good. The best *souvlaki* is flavoured subtly with herbs. Roast lamb *(arnaki psito)* and roast kid *(katsiki sto fourno)* are not always available, but can be had in rural tavernas during festivals. And for the adventurous, how about *kokoretsi* – lamb liver, heart, kidney and tripe kebab…

FISH

Fish, as always, is expensive, but there is nothing better than fresh fish in a good *psarotaverna* (fish restaurant) or beachside venue. Try *marides* for starters; this is whitebait, fried whole in olive oil, sprinkled with lemon and accompanied by greens. Then there is a Greek favourite, *kalamari*, fried squid; or the Italian-influenced *bianco*, a casserole of whiting, Scorpion fish, or grey mullet cooked in garlic, pepper and lemon juice. Try *bourdetto*, a selection of small fish, oven-cooked in a sauce of oil, garlic, tomato, spring onion and red pepper. A cheaper option is *xsifhia*, a kind of 'fish-kebab', with pieces of grilled swordfish sharing a skewer with tomato and onion. Lobster *(astakos)* is the ultimate treat, but it's expensive.

DRINK

Ouzo is the great Greek drink for socialising, and the essential appetizer to a feast. At nearly 50 per cent alcohol, and with a strong aniseed flavour, it can shrivel the palate of the uninitiated. Take sparingly, with water and some ice.

Greek wines are often dismissed, but they have kept the Greeks smiling and singing for a long time. As long as you are not an ostentatious cork-sniffer, you'll find some good wines on Corfu. These include Santa Domenica, light white and red, made from *kakotrygis* grapes.

Some tavernas make their own wine, *varelisio*, from the barrel and this can be extremely good. Small rural vintners produce distinctive wines such as Liapáditiko, a white wine produced in the Liapádes area, near Paleokastritsa. Corfu's most famous wine is the expensive and elusive Theotoki Roppa.

Retsina is a good stand-by. This is resinated wine, common throughout Greece; an acquired taste, but when it is good and from the barrel, it is persuasive; when it is bad, usually from the bottle, it can be wicked. Light beers and lagers are a standard drink throughout Greece.

The Greeks know well that coffee-drinking makes philosophers or gossips of us all. For a safe, familiar drink, 'Nescafé' is universally recognized as meaning instant coffee. Try *Ellinikos kafes* (Greek coffee), made from thick grounds, served in tiny cups, either *sketo* (unsweetened), *metrio* (medium sweet) or *gliko* (sweetened). Do not swallow in one gulp. Sip gently. It comes with a glass of water, which can be added in small portions to settle the grounds. Try too, *kafes frappe*, a long glass of smooth, iced coffee, sweetened or unsweetened, again accompanied by a glass of water.

You can ask for tea *(tsa-i)*, but it's not always available. If it is, make it clear if you want milk *(gala)* or sugar *(zahari)* with it. Orange juice in the best cafés is made from fresh oranges, and is delicious. Soft drinks *(anapsiktika)* are available in universal brands. Greek soft drinks, such as *portokalada* (fizzy orange) and lemon-flavoured *limonadha,* are very sweet.

Ginger beer, or *tsin tsin birra,* to give it the proper Corfiot name, is still available on Corfu and can be bought in the Liston cafés. A legacy of the British Protectorate, the drink is made in traditional fashion using the finest ingredients of grated ginger, lemon juice, lemon oil, water and sugar. The mix is brewed in large cauldrons and is best taken fresh, although, traditionally, it was stored for long periods in stone bottles sealed with glass marble stoppers and kept in the cool waters of island wells.

DESSERTS

If you 'eat Greek', you rarely have room left for such indulgences as dessert. Restaurants have a dessert menu and most tavernas will have something on offer, including fresh fruit, the best way to finish a meal; or, you could ask for the lip-smacking *giaourti kai meli,* yoghurt with honey.

Alternatively, if you are eating in Corfu Town, move on to a *zaharoplastio,* a word which translates marvellously as 'sugar-sculptor'. This is a café-pâtisserie, where you can indulge in a feast of *kataifi* (wheat cakes soaked in honey); or *baklava* (nut and syrup cake); or *loukoumades* (fritters soaked in honey).

short break

If you have only a short time to visit Corfu and would like to take home some unforgettable memories you can do something local and capture the real flavour of the island. The following suggestions will give you a wide range of sights and experiences that won't take very long, won't cost very much and will make your visit very special. If you only have time to choose just one of these, you will have found the heart of the island.

● **Explore Corfu Town** (➤ 81–106). Absorb the hectic buzz of modern San Rocco Square, then stroll northeast along Georgiou Theotoki and Voulgareos streets, with side steps into the shaded alleyways of the Campiello (Old Town; ➤ 42–43), before bursting out into the sunshine and open space of the Spianáda (Esplanade).

- **Walk along a track** through peaceful olive groves, on the hills, or above the sea. The best walking areas are on the more remote northeast and west coasts, and on the high ground of Mount Pandokrator (➤ 54–55), Mount Ágios Matthéos (➤ 170) and Mount Ágios Déka. However, by walking inland through olive groves, peace and quiet can also be found within a few metres of busy resorts. Of interest to any walking enthusiast is the Corfu Trail, a 200km (124-mile) fully marked walk crossing the whole island.

- **Eat out** at a top-quality village or beach taverna where good Greek food is served, such as Stamatis at Virós (➤ 59), or Maestro at Acharávi (➤ 143). Be talkative, be lively. Indulge yourself.

- **Swim** ...and swim again...and again...and again in brilliant blue sea...

● **Live a little nightlife,** depending on your taste. Try the sound and light shows in the Old Citadel, a Greek evening in a taverna, a blitz of sound at any of the resort clubs or on the disco strip on Eth Antistasseos on the coast road to the northwest of Corfu Town.

● **Take a boat trip** round the coast, out to the Diapondía Islands (➤ 154) or Paxos (➤ 100). A view from the sea increases familiarity with Corfu.

- **Visit one of Corfu's** inland villages, such as Doukádes(➤ 154–155), Ágios Matthéos (➤ 170), Lefkímmi (➤ 177) or Sinarádes (➤ 182). Wander freely, but discreetly, into authentic Corfu.

- **Visit at least some** of Corfu Town's historic, religious and cultural sites, such as Ágios Spyrídonas (Church of St Spyrídon; ➤ 38–39).

- **Climb Mount Pandokrator** (➤ 54–55) or Mount Ágios Matthéos (➤ 170), but go as early in the day as possible.

- **Visit Paleokastritsa** (➤ 52–53) for its dramatic coastal and mountain landscape, its delightful beaches, absorbing monastery, and the hilltop ruin of Angelókastro (➤ 40–41).

Planning

Before You Go

WHEN TO GO

JAN	FEB	MAR	APR	MAY	JUN	JUL	AUG	SEP	OCT	NOV	DEC
14°C	15°C	16°C	19°C	23°C	28°C	31°C	32°C	28°C	23°C	19°C	16°C
57°F	59°F	61°F	66°F	73°F	82°F	88°F	90°F	82°F	73°F	66°F	61°F

🔵 High season ⚪ Low season

May and June are good times to visit, when the temperature starts to climb but it isn't too hot and the island is not yet too busy with visitors. Those interested in wild flowers, and who don't mind the risk of occasional showers, should consider April. In July and August it is hot and there is very little rain, although even then you may get some showers. Corfu is one of the greenest of the Greek islands, and it can rain at any time. The holiday season runs from Easter until October, and outside this period many hotels and restaurants will be closed. There are still many open all year round, but your choices will be more limited. Corfu does not make for a good winter holiday, although Corfu Town provides an under-rated city break destination.

WHAT YOU NEED

● Required
○ Suggested
▲ Not required

Some countries require a passport to remain valid for a minimum period (usually at least six months) beyond the date of entry – contact their consulate or embassy or your travel agent for details.

	UK	Germany	USA	Netherlands	Spain
Passport (or National Identity Card where applicable)	●	●	●	●	▲
Visa (regulations can change – check before you travel)	▲	▲	▲	▲	▲
Onward or Return Ticket	▲	▲	●	▲	▲
Health Inoculations (tetanus and polio)	○	○	○	○	○
Health Documentation (➤ 23, Health Advice)	●	●	▲	●	▲
Travel Insurance	●	●	●	●	●
Driving Licence (national)	●	●	●	●	●
Car Insurance Certificate	●	●	●	●	●
Car Registration Document	●	●	●	●	●

ADVANCE PLANNING
WEBSITES
- www.culture.gr
- www.gnto.gr
- www.ktel.org
- www.corfuonline.gr
- www.greeka.com/ionian/corfu/island/travel-corfu.htm
- www.agni.gr
- www.corfunews.net
- www.pelekas.com

TOURIST OFFICES AT HOME
In the UK Greek National Tourist Organisation (GNTO) ✉ 4 Conduit Street, London, W1R 0DJ
☎ 020 7734 5997
In the USA Greek National Tourist Organisation (GNTO) ✉ Olympic Tower, 645 5th Avenue, New York, NY 10022 ☎ 212/421-5777
In Canada Greek National Tourism Organisation (GNTO) ✉ 91 Scollard Street, Toronto, Ontario, M5R 1GR
☎ 416/968-2220
In Australia Greek National Tourism Organisation (GNTO) ✉ 51–57 Pitt Street, Sydney, NSW 2000 ☎ (02) 9241 1663

HEALTH ADVICE
Insurance Visitors from EU countries are entitled to reciprocal state medical care in Greece and should take an EHIC – European Health Insurance Card. However, this covers treatment in only the most basic of hospitals and private medical insurance is advisable.

Dental services Dental treatment must be paid for by all visitors. Hotels can normally provide you with the name of a local English-speaking dentist; alternatively you could ask the Tourist Police or a tourist office. Private medical insurance is strongly advisable to cover dental treatment.

TIME DIFFERENCES

GMT 12 noon	Corfu 2PM	Germany 1PM	USA (NY) 7AM	Netherlands 1PM	Spain 1PM

Corfu, like the whole of Greece, is two hours ahead of Greenwich Mean Time (GMT+2) and adjusts to summertime at 4am on the last Sunday in March until 4am on the last Sunday in October.

WHAT'S ON WHEN

January 1 January – *New Year's Day.*
6 January – *Epiphany*. Religious ceremonies held.

February–March *Pre-Lenten Carnival*. During the three weeks before the start of Lent, carnivals take place at various villages on Corfu. On the Sunday before Lent (seven Sundays before Easter) there is a big carnival procession in Corfu Town.
Kathari Deftera (Clean Monday) – the Monday after Carnival Sunday and before Ash Wednesday. Public holiday in Greece. On Corfu it is celebrated by families and friends with huge picnics. Kite flying.
8 March – *St Theodora's Day*. The saint's remains are carried around Corfu Town.
25 March – *Independence Day* and *Feast of the Annunciation*.

April *Easter* (movable). The most important celebration of the Greek year. A genuine rebirth. On Corfu, numerous religious services are held during the preceding Holy Week.
Palm Sunday – the remains of St Spyrídon are carried in procession through Corfu Town.
Good Friday – numerous church processions through Corfu Town and at villages.
Easter Saturday – procession from Church of St Spyrídon. Pot throwing custom (➤ opposite). Atmospheric late evening candle-lit ceremony of the Resurrection on the Esplanade. Fireworks display.
Easter Sunday – Resurrection parades from churches in Corfu Town and villages. Countless fairs. throughout the island.

May 1 May – *Labour day*. Festival at Róda and on Mount Ágios Déka, and family picnics throughout the island.
4 May – *Feast of St Thomas*. festivals at Sidári, Gastoúri and Benítses, among others.
8 May – festival at Kassiópi.
21 May – *Ionian Day*. Annual celebration of the Ionian Islands union with Greece in 1864. Local holiday. Procession in Corfu Town. Brass band display on the Esplanade.

NATIONAL HOLIDAYS

JAN	FEB	MAR	APR	MAY	JUN	JUL	AUG	SEP	OCT	NOV	DEC
2	(1)	1(2)	(1)	1	1		1		1		2

1 Jan	New Year's Day
6 Jan	Epiphany
End Feb/early Mar	*Kathari Deftera* (Clean Monday)
25 Mar	Independence Day
Mar/Apr	Holy Week Celebrations
1 May	Labour Day
3 Jun	Holy Spirit Day
15 Aug	Feast of the Assumption
28 Oct	Óchi Day
25 Dec, 26 Dec	Christmas Day, St Stephen's Day

The Feast of St Spyridon (11 Aug) is an unofficial public holiday. Shops and some restaurants close on public holidays. In Corfu Town and in main resorts, tavernas and most shops stay open.

June *Pentecost Sunday* – festival at Lákones.
Whit Monday – festivals at Kondókali, Stavros and Argirádes, among others.

July 8 July – *St Prokopios's Day.* Festival at Lefkímmi.
26 July – *St Paraskevi's Day.* Festivals at Ágios Matthéos, Ipsos, Avliótes, Benítses, Kinopiastes.

August 6 August – *Saviour's Day.* During the preceding week there are pilgrimages to the top of Mount Pandokrator (► 54–55). Festivals in Campiello district of Corfu Town, Ágios Matthéos and Strinýlas.
11 August – *St Spyrídon's Day.* Big procession of casket holding saint's remains through Corfu Town.

15 August – *Assumption of the Virgin.* National holiday. Corfiots traditionally return to home villages. Festivals at Platitéra Monastery (► 105) and at numerous villages.

Pot throwing

At 11am on Holy Saturday morning the custom of pot throwing takes place, involving large earthenware pots, sometimes filled with water, being dropped from windows and high balconies in Corfu Town. Pots are also smashed in villages. There are numerous explanations, ranging from it being a reference to Judas's betrayal of Christ for a pot of gold, to the joy of the Virgin Mary at discovering Christ's tomb to be empty, to prehistoric rituals of pottery breaking at burials.

Getting There

BY AIR

There are no direct scheduled flights to Corfu from airports outside Greece although rumours are always rife about various carriers being 'in discussion' about establishing a direct service from one or other Northern European airport, including British ones. It is worth checking general flight websites to see whether or not this much rumoured service has become a reality.

Scheduled services Current scheduled services operate via Athens where they connect with the regular daily internal flights to the island. These take about 1 hour and are operated by the Greek national carrier, Olympic Airways (☎ 26610-38694; **www.**olympic-airways.gr) or the privately operated Aegean Airlines (☎ 26610-27100; **www.**aegeanair.com). Olympic also operates three flights per week between Corfu and Greece's second city, Thessaloníki.

Seaplanes A seaplane service, run by AirSea Lines (☎ 26610-49800 Corfu Town; 26610-99316 Gouviá Marina; **www.**airsealines.com) using 19-seater De Havilland Twin

Otters, operates daily flights between Igoumenítsa on the Greek mainland and Gouviá in Corfu. The company also operates daily flights between Gouviá and Paxos. At the time of writing, future developments included the possibility of flights between Corfu and Brindisi in Italy.

Charter flights In the summer holiday season there are numerous direct charter flights from many European countries to Corfu, the season usually running from Easter until October.

Holiday companies will offload unsold charter flights via the internet or high-street travel agents,

Pátras on the Greek mainland, which is a useful connection if combining a visit to Corfu with other parts of Greece.

The most regular services from the Greek mainland are from Igoumenítsa to Corfu Town, with at least one car ferry per hour during the day, all year round, and even more frequently in summer. The journey takes under 2 hours on the larger ferries and just over an hour on the smaller ones.

There are also the more expensive passenger-only Flying Dolphin hydrofoils which make the trip in 40 minutes. There are less frequent ferries from Igoumenítsa to Lefkímmi in southern Corfu with a journey-time of one hour.

and it is fairly easy to pick up cheap flights to Corfu outside the peak summer months. In July and August flight availability will depend on how well holiday bookings are going that year.

Corfu Airport (☎ 26610-30180) is about 3km (2 miles) to the south of Corfu Town (Kérkyra).

For general ferry schedules, **www.**gtp.gr is a good website.

It's 1.5km (1 mile) from New Port Ferry Terminal to Corfu Town.

BY SEA

There are ferry connections to Corfu from five ports in Italy, including Venice, but the closest and most frequent services are from Brindisi.

BY BUS

Getting to an island by bus might not seem the obvious option, but there are daily bus services from Athens to Corfu, which take about 10–11 hours and reach the island on the ferry service from the mainland port at Igoumenítsa.

Some of these Italian ferries stop at Corfu on their journey to and from

Getting Around

DRIVING

Driving is on the right. Speed limit on national highways: **100kph (62mph)**. Outside built-up areas: **90kph (56mph)**. Built-up areas: **50kph (31mph)**. Seatbelts must be worn in front seats and in the rear where fitted. Children under 10 years are not allowed in the front seat. Random breath testing takes place. Never drive under the influence of alcohol.

Super and unleaded petrol and diesel are all available. There are few petrol stations in rural areas and they tend to be the most expensive. They open daily (morning only) but may close on Sunday. Cash payment is preferred in rural stations. A useful word is *yemitse* (fill).

It is compulsory to carry a first-aid kit, a fire extinguisher and a warning triangle. Tourists with proof of AA/RAC or similar membership are given free roadside assistance from ELPA, the Greek motoring club. If your vehicle breaks down, dial 104. There are good repair shops in big towns but in rural areas petrol stations can usually find a local mechanic.

INTERNAL FLIGHTS

Domestic flights are operated by Olympic Airways (☎ 26610-38694; **www.**olympic-airlines.com) and Aegean Airlines (☎ 26610-27100; **www.**aegeanair.com), and it is possible to make connections at Athens to Corfu. A seaplane service, run by AirSea Lines operates from Gouviá Marina to Igoumenítsa on the mainland and from Gouviá to Paxos (➤ 26).

ISLAND BUSES

Corfu's rural bus service is run by the national bus company, KTEL (Kratiko Tamio Ellinikon Leoforion). All services start from and return to

Corfu Town. Timetables may be subject to change. Buses can be boarded anywhere along country roads, and tickets are purchased on board. KTEL buses also run between Corfu and Athens. The KTEL terminus in Corfu Town is at the northwest end of Avramiou. For more information ☎ 26610-30627/39985.

FERRIES

Ferries run between Corfu Town and Igoumenítsa on the mainland at half-hourly intervals in winter, and as frequently as 15-minute intervals in summer. Ferries also run at hourly intervals between Lefkímmi and Igoumenítsa. International ferries run between Bari and Brindisi in Italy and Patras on the Greek mainland, calling at Corfu Town. Ferry connections between Corfu and Paxos are uncertain and should be checked.

URBAN TRANSPORT

Blue buses (☎ 26610-39859) operate from San Rocco Square to the suburbs and Gastoúri (Achilleion), Kondókali, Gouviá, Dassiá, Pérama, Benítses, Pélekas, Kanóni, and central Corfu. Pay on board or, for buses marked *horis eispraktor* (without conductor) buy tickets at the kiosk by the San Rocco bus rank.

TAXIS

Call radio cabs (☎ 26610-33811/2). Taxi ranks in Corfu Town are at San Rocco Square, the Esplanade and New Port. Meters should display the fare; if not make sure you determine the cost beforehand. Double rates apply outside Corfu Town.

CAR AND MOTORCYCLE RENTAL

Make sure you have Collision Damage Waiver. However, even

with CDW you are liable for damage to tyres and undercarriage, so do not drive conventional vehicles off-road. Always check the wheels, bodywork and interior of the vehicle in the presence of the hirer before accepting the vehicle. If there is existing damage, make sure that the hirer acknowledges this. Visitors are strongly advised not to consume any alcohol if intending to drive. The minimum rental age is from 21 to 25.

Being There

TOURIST OFFICES
Visitors should note that Greek National Tourism Organization (GNTO) is the title used outside Greece. In Greece it is known as Ellinikos Organismos Tourismou (EOT).

ATHENS
● Greek National Tourism Organization (GNTO), Head Office Tsoha 7, Ambelokipi, Athens 11521 ☎ (210) 870 7000

● GNTO Central Information Office, Amalias 26a, Syntagma, Athens ☎ (210) 331 0392

CORFU TOURIST INFORMATION
● The EOT has closed its Corfu Town office and currently has an office outside town on Eth Antistasseos, which has little information. Tourist information kisoks may be opened in Corfu Town but details are not confirmed at time of writing. Website: **www.**gnto.gr

The Tourist Police (☎ 26610-30265) should be contacted if visitors have difficulties with accommodation or with service.

A friendly reliable agency in Corfu Town that will give some information and arrange accommodation, tours and more for a fee is: **All Ways Travel,** 35 G Theotoki Square ☎ 26610-33955

EMBASSIES AND CONSULATES
UK ☎ 26610-30055/23457
USA/Canada ☎ (210) 721 2951 (Athens)
Germany ☎ 26610-31453
Australia ☎ (210) 645 0404 (Athens)
Netherlands ☎ 26610-39900
Italy ☎ 26610-37351

EMAIL AND INTERNET
Corfu Town has several internet cafés including Netoikos, 14 Kaloxairetou (behind The Liston) ☎ 26610-28637 and Café Online, 28 Kapodistriou (just up from Arcadion Hotel) ☎ 26610-46226. A few of the larger resorts also have internet cafés, usually open until midnight or 1am.

TELEPHONES
To make a call from a street phone you must have an OTE (the national phone company) phone card *(telekarte)*. These can be bought for

OPENING HOURS

- Shops
- Banks
- Museums/Monuments
- Offices
- Post Offices
- Pharmacies

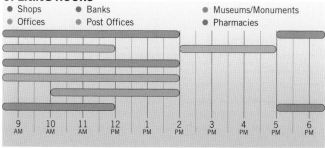

| 9 AM | 10 AM | 11 AM | 12 PM | 1 PM | 2 PM | 3 PM | 4 PM | 5 PM | 6 PM |

In addition to the above times (a guide only), supermarkets and gift shops, particularly in resorts, often stay open until 9 or 10pm.

Pharmacies are closed on Saturday and Sunday. Check opening times of museums and sites locally as they vary from summer to winter.

a few euros at small local shops, souvenir shops and, chiefly, at *periptera*, the street kiosks that sell everything from cigarettes to magazines. You can also use the OTE office in Corfu Town (Mantzarou 3), which is better value for international calls. Travel agencies in smaller towns often offer direct dialing facilities. For the domestic operator dial 151, and for the international operator dial 161.

EMERGENCY TELEPHONE NUMBERS
Police 100
Fire 199
Forest fire 191
Ambulance 166
Tourist police 26610-30265

INTERNATIONAL DIALLING CODES
Dial 00 followed by:
UK: 44
USA/Canada: 1
Ireland: 353
Australia: 61
Germany: 49

POSTAL SERVICES
The main post office in Corfu Town is at the junction of Alexandras and Zafiropoulou streets; it's open Mon–Fri 7.30am–8pm.

TOILETS
There are very few public toilets in Corfu. Tavernas and restaurants must have them by law.

ELECTRICITY
The power supply throughout Greece is 220 volts AC, 50 Hz. Sockets accept two-round-pin Continental-style plugs. Visitors from the UK will need a plug adaptor and US visitors will need a voltage transformer.

CURRENCY AND FOREIGN EXCHANGE
Currency The monetary unit in Corfu and throughout Greece is the euro (€). Notes are in denominations of €5, 10, 20, 50, 100, 200 and 500, with coins for 1 and 2 euros, and 1, 2, 5, 10, 20 and 50 cents.

Exchange Cash and travellers' cheques can be exchanged in banks, at exchange bureaux and often in travel agencies and tourist information centres. In small resorts the travel agencies may be your only option as there are only banks in Corfu Town and some of the larger resorts. Banks generally give better exchange rates although commission charges are not standardized so shop around for the best deal. Post offices in Greece no longer offer currency exchange facilities.

Credit cards These are widely accepted in hotels, shops and many restaurants, but a few of the eating places recommended in this guide will only take cash so don't rely totally on plastic. You will need a credit card if you wish to rent a car. There are ATMs in all major resorts, but if staying in a smaller place it is wise to check first.

HEALTH AND SAFETY
Sun advice During the months of May to September, when the sun

TIPS/GRATUITIES

Yes ✓   No ✗

Restaurants (service included)	✓	10% or change
Cafés/bars (if service not included)	✓	10%
Taxis	✓	change
Tour guides	✓	€4
Porters	✓	€2 per bag
Chambermaids	✓	discretionary
Restroom attendants	✓	50 cents
Hairdressers	✓	10%

is at its hottest, a hat, strong-protection suncream and plenty of water are recommended. Try to keep out of the midday sun.

Drugs Prescription and non-prescription drugs are widely available at pharmacies, indicated by a Green Cross, and they usually have someone who can speak English. When closed each should carry a notice of the nearest open pharmacy, or ring 107 to find out. Bring sufficient supplies of any medication with you, especially if staying in smaller resorts. Also bring prescriptions, indicating generic and not brand names, in case you need more. Codeine is banned in Greece, so check your medical supplies to avoid falling foul of the law.

Safe water Tap water is chlorinated and is regarded as safe.

PHOTOGRAPHY
What to photograph: ancient sites (photography is free for hand held cameras on most sites), villages, parades, harbours. The Greek people like being photographed, but it is polite to ask permission. Where you need permission: in some museums and always if using a tripod. Never photograph near military installations.

CLOTHING SIZES

France	UK	Rest of Europe	USA	
46	36	46	36	
48	38	48	38	
50	40	50	40	
52	42	52	42	
54	44	54	44	Suits
56	46	56	46	
41	7	41	8	
42	7.5	42	8.5	
43	8.5	43	9.5	
44	9.5	44	10.5	
45	10.5	45	11.5	Shoes
46	11	46	12	
37	14.5	37	14.5	
38	15	38	15	
39/40	15.5	39/40	15.5	
41	16	41	16	
42	16.5	42	16.5	Shirts
43	17	43	17	
36	8	34	6	
38	10	36	8	
40	12	38	10	
42	14	40	12	
44	16	42	14	Dresses
46	18	44	16	
38	4.5	38	6	
38	5	38	6.5	
39	5.5	39	7	
39	6	39	7.5	
40	6.5	40	8	Shoes
41	7	41	8.5	

Best places to see

1 Achilleío (Achilleion Palace)

Corfu's famous Achilleion Palace is an entertaining example of rather florid neoclassicism and self-indulgence, but all of it set within beautiful surroundings.

The Achilleion, a fascinating relic of 19th-century grand design and occasional kitsch, stands on tree-clad heights above the east coast resort of

Benítses, adjacent to the village of Gastoúri. It was conceived by the Empress Elizabeth of Austria as a tribute to her spiritual hero Achilles, and the result is a confection of colonnades and stucco work based on the classical elegance of Pompeii, the whole crowded with statues, paintings and 19th-century furnishings. Six years after the palace was completed in 1892, the Empress was killed by an assassin on the quayside of Lake Geneva. In 1908 the palace was bought by Kaiser Wilhelm II, who added his own grandiose touches before leaving Corfu in 1914 for more pressing engagements. Eventually taken over by the Greek state, the Achilleion lay unused until it was converted into a casino in 1963.

On view is the ornately decorated entrance hall, the Empress's chapel, and ground-floor reception rooms containing furnishings and memorabilia of the Empress and the Kaiser. In the terraced gardens are numerous statues including the Empress's favourite, the sentimental 'Dying Achilles', and the Kaiser's contribution, an outrageously monumental 'Achilles Triumphant'.

✚ 31P ✉ Gastoúri village. Signposted from Corfu Town and from the coast road north of Benítses ☎ 26610-56245 🕐 Jun–Aug daily 9–7; Sep–May daily 9–3.30 ✋ Expensive 🍴 Cafés (€€) near entrance 🚌 Blue bus 10 from San Rocco Square, Corfu Town ❓ Limited roadside parking only. Very crowded during Jul and Aug

2 Ágios Spyrídonas (Church of St Spyrídon)

Ágios Spyrídonas is the most famous church in Corfu. Built in 1590 to house the sacred relics of St Spyrídon, the patron saint of Corfu and a focus of devotion on the island, where he is known simply as 'The Saint', it is a place of pilgrimage to this day.

Spyrídon (AD270–c348) was a Cypriot bishop, said to have performed numerous miracles. During the 7th century, the saint's revered remains were transferred from Cyprus to Constantinople, but, on the fall of the city in 1453, his body was brought, eventually, to Corfu by an itinerant priest. St Spyrídon is associated with several events which are said to have saved the island from plague, famine and Turkish siege and these are celebrated with solemn, but colourful, processions in which his remains are carried through Corfu Town.

The tall, red-domed bell-tower of the Church of St Spyrídon, reminiscent of the tower of San Giorgio dei Greci in Venice, is a landmark of central Corfu Town. Plain exterior walls hide a lavish interior: there is a superb iconostasis (a screen of white Cycladian marble); silver thuribles (censers) and candelabra crowd the basilica; and a wealth of paintings and icons decorate the walls.

In spite of the steady procession of the faithful – and the merely curious – which passes across the pink-and-white flagstones and through the doors to either side, there is a subdued atmosphere inside the church. Candles still flicker

in the gloom 'like yellow crocuses', as described by Gerald Durrell in his reminiscences of a Corfu childhood. Young and old, the plain and the fashionable pay homage to the saint.

The real focus of the church, however, is the ornate casket containing the mummified remains of the saint. These are exposed annually on 12 December (St Spyrídon's Day), at Easter, and on 11 August. The saint's feet are clad in embroidered slippers, which devotees claim become worn because of Spyrídon's frequent night-time wanderings round the Old Town. The casket, silver-coated and bearing 12 enamel medallions, is situated to the right of the altar, within a separate chapel, beneath lamps and votive offerings from which dangle tiny silver ships and other motifs. Only a few steps take you from the dazzling sunshine of the outside world into this intense focus of Greek Orthodoxy.

✚ *Kérkyra 3e* ✉ Ayiou Spiridonas Street, Corfu Town. Also reached from Plateía Iroon Kypriakou Agonos (St Spyrídon's Square) 🕐 Daily 9–2. Casual visits during services are best avoided ✋ Free, donations welcome 🍴 Café Plakada (€€) in St Spyrídon's Square ❓ Sober clothing should be worn

3 Angelókastro

The 12th-century ruin of the Byzantine fortress of Angelókastro occupies a spectacular hilltop on the west coast.

Angelókastro is one of the finest historic sites on Corfu. Fortified in the 12th century, it may later have been named after the Byzantine family of Angeloi Komneni, which ruled Corfu during the 11th and 12th centuries. The fortress played a key role in the successful defence of the island for hundreds of years, as from it, a watch could be kept on the vulnerable west coast and signals exchanged with Corfu Town. Angelókastro's greatest test came when several thousand islanders withstood sieges by Turkish invaders in 1537, 1571 and 1716. Its military use ended in the 19th century during the British Protectorate.

The ruins of the fortress stand on top of a rocky pinnacle whose cliffs drop 300m (985ft) into the sea. Cobbled steps wind steeply from a car park to a narrow entrance into the inner keep, above which is the upper keep, crowned by the tiny Church of the Archangels Michael and Gabriel.

Just east of the summit, and at a lower level, are the remains of underground water cisterns. In the lower keep, on the far left of the entrance, is a remarkable hermitage – a cave that was converted into a chapel to St Kyriaki in the late 18th century. Wall-paintings of the Virgin and Christ survive.

🔒 3A ✉ Kríni, just west of Makrádes (follow signs) and 28km (17 miles) from Corfu Town 🕐 May–Sep daily 8.30–3 🍴 Castelo St Angelo Taverna (€€) beside car park 🚌 Green bus from Avramiou Street, Corfu Town–Makrádes, then 2.5km (1.5-mile) walk ✋ Inexpensive ❓ Take care near the unprotected cliff edges. The entrance gate is halfway up the approach steps and is usually locked in winter and sometimes early and late in the season, if the ticket kiosk is unattended. Access is not feasible for those with limited mobility

4 Campiello: Old Corfu Town

The old part of Corfu Town is known as Campiello. It lies behind the seafront between the Old and New fortresses.

Venetian is the emphatic style of Campiello's buildings and its fascinating maze of narrow streets, the *kandounia*, which spreads between the main thoroughfares; lanes are often linked by stone stairways *(skalinades)*, and by vaulted passageways. The original buildings of the medieval town, which developed on the cramped peninsula as a domestic adjunct to the Old Fortress, eventually replacing it as the administrative centre of the island, are long gone. Here, the Venetians built grand Renaissance houses three or four storeys high, which were added to in later centuries to accommodate a growing population within the town walls.

Venetian motifs survive on the sometimes crumbling façades of these wonderful old buildings and on the doorcases, or *portonia*, with their distinctive mouldings. Throughout the day the sun weaves an intricate pattern of shifting light on the walls and turns them to burnished gold in the evening. In the narrow, sun-dappled canyons of Campiello, lines of washing hang like banners between the upper windows, and the mottled walls rise cliff-like past railed balconies and stone pediments to a final blue ribbon of sky. Underfoot, the ground is smoothly paved, and intriguing courtyards, terraced gardens, ancient churches and shrines appear round every other corner. There are neighbourhood shops, cafés, tavernas, bars and

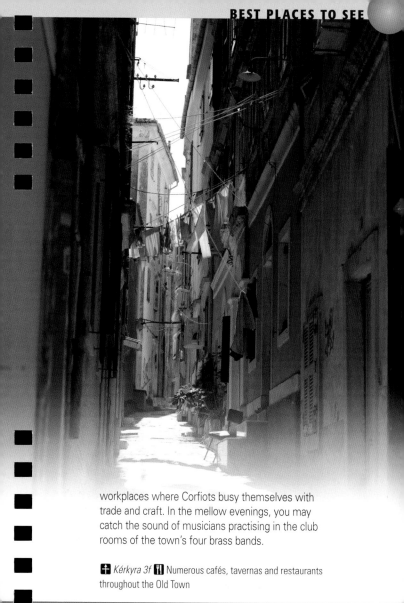

workplaces where Corfiots busy themselves with trade and craft. In the mellow evenings, you may catch the sound of musicians practising in the club rooms of the town's four brass bands.

✚ *Kérkyra 3f* 🍴 Numerous cafés, tavernas and restaurants throughout the Old Town

5 Kalámi

Kalámi lies on Corfu's northeast coast, amid a landscape of quiet bays backed by the tree-clad slopes of Mount Pandokrator.

In the famous White House at Kalámi, the writer Lawrence Durrell lived for a time and drew on his impressions for his lyrical book *Prospero's Cell*. Today, Kalámi's idyllic peace and quiet, the 'charms

of seclusion' described so vividly by Durrell, are no more. Seen from the north, its deep-blue bay caught within a green amphitheatre of cypresses and olives, the village still reflects the quintessential beauty of old Corfu. Unfortunately, the view from the south includes the modern terraced apartments that dominate the west side of the bay.

The White House, 'set like a dice on a rock already venerable with the scars of wind and water', stands on the south side of the bay. It is distinctly English-looking, with its solid, square shape and its broad, hipped roof. Here Durrell and his wife, Nancy, lived what seems to have been a truly idyllic life in the Ionian sun. Their quickest way to Corfu Town was by boat and they travelled a great deal in their little sailing boat, the *Van Norden*. Their friends were a collection of serene eccentrics. Even the dynamic Henry Miller was persuaded to visit for a time and was captivated by Greece. The fruit of this was Miller's splendid book *The Colossus of Maroussi*. Today, the White House functions as a restaurant with apartments above.

Kalámi has a number of other tavernas, interspersed with villas, the whole softened by groves of orange and lemon trees, olives and cypresses. Although the resort is busy in summer, it is quiet in the evenings. Boats can be rented, and the beach is very safe for children.

➕ 10C ✉ 1km (0.5 miles) off the main coast road, 30km (19 miles) north of Corfu Town 🍴 The White House (€€) 🚌 Green bus from Avramiou Street, Corfu Town–Kassiópi/Loútses. Walk from main road ⛴ Small ferry boats from nearby resorts ❓ Limited parking

6 Kanóni

The resort lies at the southern tip of the Kanóni Peninsula overlooking the two little islands of Vlachérna and Pontikonísi (Mouse Island).

The view of Vlachérna, with its little convent and its solitary cypress tree, and of Pontikonísi, with its thicket of trees and its chapel, is probably the most photographed in the Ionian Islands, an enduring visual symbol of modern Corfu. The sounds accompanying this scenic delight are less soothing: Corfu's airport runway slices across the adjoining lagoon, Chalkiopoúlou, a few hundred metres away. (Youngsters will love plane-spotting.)

There is precedent for sound and fury, however. Kanóni is so named from being the site of a gun battery, first established by the French during the British blockade of Corfu from 1810 to 1815. Today, a Russian cannon, installed about 30 years ago, stands on the viewing terrace overlooking Vlachérna and Pontikonísi. Winding steps lead down from the terrace to the small harbour, from where Vlachérna is reached along a causeway. The Convent of the Virgin Mary here has a fine Venetian belfry. Boats ferry visitors to Pontikonísi and run to and from Corfu Town. The Byzantine Church of Pandokrator on Pontikonísi, is said to date from the 11th or 12th century.

✚ 32R ✉ At the southernmost tip of the Kanóni Peninsula,
5km (3 miles) south of Corfu Town 🍴 Kanoni (€–€€) 🚌 2
Kanóni. Blue bus from San Rocco Square 🚢 Caique ferries
to and from Corfu Town ❓ Follow parking signs on
approach road and branch right, signed Pontikonísi, to reach
harbourside car park. There is a one-way traffic system
round the tip of the Kanóni Peninsula, so keep a sharp
lookout for the Pontikonísi sign. If you miss it, you cannot
turn back and are left with very limited parking beside the
viewing terrace and café

7 Límni Korissión (Lake Korissión)

Southwest Corfu is low-lying, a gentle foil to the mountainous north. Typical of the area is Lake Korissión, a large expanse of water that lies on the scimitar curve of the coast behind the remote Halikounas Beach.

Lake Korissión is a man-made lagoon of 607ha (1,500 acres), created by the Venetians, who constructed a short, reinforced channel from the sea and flooded existing marshlands. It offers a peaceful respite from crowded beaches and the more popular resorts. Inland, the lake is bordered by low hills and, to the north, Mount Ágios Matthéos looms large. Even the ever-present olive relents here, to be replaced by silvery-green juniper and cedar trees that lie scattered along the lake shores. Flowering plants at Korissión include the spring catchfly, or loose-flowered orchid, with its purple blooms, just one of the dozen or so orchid species that flourish here. Summer sees the blue-

green sea holly and various spurges, and later in the season, the white flowers of the sand lily.

The lake and its margins provide an ideal winter habitat for birds. Over 120 species have been recorded, including rare migrants such as the great white egret and the glossy ibis. Overwintering visitors include mallard, shelduck and teal.

The neck of the channel at the entrance to the lake is blocked with fish traps to control the passage and catching of grey mullet – a rough track runs down the seaward edge of the lake from its northern end to a fish-watcher's hut beside the channel. One of the charms of Lake Korissión is its remoteness, and it has the bonus of a stretch of sandy beach north and south of the channel, although the lake area and adjoining beach can become crowded and noisy at the height of the summer season and on holiday weekends. You can walk south along the beach to escape it all.

✚ 17K ✉ On the west coast about 20km (12.5 miles) south of Corfu Town ❚❚ Taverna (€) at north end of lake ❓ The north end of the lake is reached by following signposts for Gardíki from a junction about 1km (0.5 miles) south of Moraïtika. The south end is reached by turning west off the main road to Kávos, at Línia, and following signs for Paralía tou Íssou (Issos Beach)

8 Mouseío Archaiologikó (Archaeological Museum)

Corfu Town's small, but rewarding, Archaeological Museum houses some outstanding relics from the island's ancient past.

The museum contains one of the finest prehistoric relics in all of Greece, the famous Gorgon pediment recovered from the ruins of the 6th-century BC Temple of Artemis on the Kanóni Peninsula. Though it is not intact, the pediment, 17m (56ft) long and 3m (10ft) high, has been restored skilfully. Such monumental antiquity may seem incidental to

devoted beach lovers, but the impact of the snake-haired, eye-popping Medusa sheltering her blood offspring, Chrysaor and Pegasus, is enough to excite the most jaded of onlookers, as she looms above, attended by Zeus and slaughtered Titans and flanked by leopards.

The Gorgon frieze is matched, in the South Hall, by the splendid Lion of Menekrates, a limestone sculpture of the late 7th century BC. Discovered in 1843, it is considered to be one of the finest examples of early Corinthian art.

Other delights include some excellent tomb monuments, classical pottery and Bronze Age artefacts, and an impressive collection of coins dating from the 6th to 3rd centuries BC. In the North Hall there are some splendid terracotta fittings and artefacts from the ruins of a 7th-century temple found in the grounds of Mon Repos villa (▶ 88).

The finest exhibit here is the left side of a limestone pediment featuring the god Dionysus and a naked youth, well supplied with wine and reclining on a couch. Both are avidly watching a scene on the lost half of the pediment, a tantalizing omission for the rest of us.

✚ *Kérkyra 2c* ✉ 5 Vraila Armeni Street ☎ 26610-30680 🕐 Tue–Sun 8.30–3 ✋ Moderate. Free on Sun 🍴 Cafés and tavernas in nearby San Rocco Square (€) and on the Liston (€€€) ❓ Photography, without flash, is permitted for some exhibits. Please check with attendants

9 Palaiokastrítsa (Paleokastritsa)

The wooded headlands and crescent-shaped bays of Corfu's most celebrated scenic extravaganza have attracted visitors since the early 19th century.

At Paleokastritsa, towering mountains give way reluctantly to the sea, their tree-clad slopes mottled with great cliffs. Here, the landscape has overwhelmed the human element, instead of the other way round, although in high summer the resort itself is very busy. Roads end at Paleokastritsa, giving a real sense of arrival.

Long before the British holidaymaker first picnicked at 'Paleo', the western headland was home to a **monastery** dedicated to the Virgin Mary. The original foundation was 13th-century, but the present complex is mainly 18th-century. A small church lies at the heart of the monastery, its walls laden with icons in chunky rococo frames; a fine painting of the Last Judgement hangs above the south doorway. From the garden terrace there is a breathtaking view across the Bay of Liapádes to Cape Ágios Iliodoros and on to distant Cape Plaka. Within the monastery complex is a preserved oil mill and a small museum displaying icons, and a collection of shells and bones from the sea.

The less spiritual delights of Paleokastritsa include the rather cramped, sun-trap beaches of Ágios Spyrídon, which lie to either side of the main car park. The harbour and beaches at Alipo Bay lie beyond the easterly headland of St Nicholas. There

are sun-loungers and water sports equipment, and boats can be rented from the harbour. Organized boat trips visit nearby cliff grottoes and caves, and the crystal-clear seas round 'Paleo' are especially good for scuba diving.

✚ 25T ✉ On the west coast of Corfu, 25km (15.5 miles) from Corfu Town 🍴 Numerous tavernas and cafés in resort 🚌 Green bus from Avramiou Street, Corfu Town–Paleokastritsa 🚢 Boat trips to view coastal features, caves and grottoes

Monastery

🕐 8–1, 3–8 ✋ A small donation appreciated 🍴 Café-restaurant (€€) outside monastery ❓ Dress appropriately when visiting the monastery

10 Pantokrátoras (Mount Pandokrator)

The mountain's vast bulk, and its rolling hinterland of *maquis* (scrubland) dense with kermes oak, myrtle and wild flowers, creates a persuasive sense of wilderness and open space.

Pandokrator, at 906m (2,971ft) a spectacular viewpoint, was known in prehistory as Istone and by the Venetians as Monte San Salvatore. In the 14th century a church dedicated to Christ Pandocrator, 'The Almighty' or 'The All Embracing One', was built on the summit of the mountain and the name was eventually applied to the entire massif. The present buildings are 19th-century replacements of earlier structures. Today, the monastery shares the crowded summit, rather

uneasily, with a huge radio mast and various other beacons and aerials. There is a pilgrimage to the monastery on 6 August each year to celebrate the Feast of the Transfiguration.

From the north the approach is by road, through Néa (New) Períthia (► 136) and then by a track to join the summit road. The best approach, however, is from the south through Spartýlas and the village of Strinýlas. Just beyond Strinýlas, bear right at a junction and on to a good road which leads to the summit. The last kilometre, surfaced with ribbed concrete, is extremely tortuous and steep. Parking space at the summit is limited. It may be more practical, and in some ways more fitting, to walk the last section from roadside parking below the summit. Experienced hillwalkers, with proper clothing, footwear and equipment, will find off-road exploration of the mountain rewarding.

✚ 9C ✉ Dominates the northeast corner of the island, 37km (23 miles) north of Corfu Town 🍴 Café outside monastery gate ✋ Monastery free, small donation welcome ❓ Roadside parking about 1km (0.5 miles) from the summit near the junction with the track from Néa (New) Períthia, signposted Pyrgí, Róda and Kassiópi

Best things to do

Excellent restaurants

Aegli (€€–€€€)

A long-established and classy Liston restaurant. Eat underneath the arches or on the Esplanade, beneath the trees. Good Corfiot *tiss katsarolass* (casseroled food) and equally tasty fish dishes.

✉ 23 Kapodistrias, Corfu Town ☎ 26610-31949 ⏰ Lunch and dinner

Chrisomallis (€)

Traditional family-run in-town taverna. Corfiot food – *pastitsada*, *stifado*, *sofrito*, *moussaká* and grilled meats. Excellent value.

✉ 6 Nikifouro Theotoki (behind the Liston), Corfu Town ☎ 26610-30342 ⏰ All day

Du Lac (€€–€€€)

Opened in the past few years, this stylish place soon won itself a good reputation. Fine Mediterranean cuisine with international influence is the motif. Great choice of mainly Greek wines.

✉ Dafnílis. On the main road from Corfu Town north to Dassiá ☎ 26610-91783 ⏰ Dinner

Etrusco (€€€)

Svelte interiors add to the sophisticated appeal of this fine out-of-town restaurant where international cuisine with Italian influences is the style. Meat and fish are lovingly and subtly

prepared. Reservations are advised. Prices are high.
✉ Kato Korakiána, northwest of Dassiá ☎ 26610-933432 🕐 Dinner

Rex (€€–€€€)
Long-established restaurant popular with Corfiots. Adventurous
sauces, including a truly local speciality, chicken in kumquat sauce.
✉ 66 Kapodistrias, Corfu Town ☎ 26610-39649 🕐 Lunch and dinner

La Rosa di Paxos (€€)
Mihales Dahetos and his Italian wife run this delightful restaurant
overlooking the harbour of Lákka on Paxos (► 100–101). Good
choice of wines including a strong white from the family vineyard
in Antipaxos. Reservations are advisable in high season.
✉ Lákka, Paxos ☎ 26620-31470 🕐 Lunch and dinner

Stamatis (€–€€)
Popular and very friendly taverna. Should not be missed. Superb
Corfiot food, *mezes* are a feast in themselves. Great house wine
and impromptu music. It can get very busy so booking is advised.
✉ Virós (near Vrioni) ☎ 26610-39249 🕐 Dinner. Closed Sun

Taverna Agni (€€–€€€)
Famous beachside eating place, family run (Corfiot and English)
and with marvellous local cuisine. Try anchovy fillets marinated in
herb-infused olive oil and aubergine slices rolled round feta cheese
and baked in a tasty sauce.
✉ Overlooking Agni beach ☎ 26630-91142 🕐 Lunch and dinner

Venetian Well (€€–€€€)
At the Italianate heart of the Old Town. Remarkable international
menu spanning East and West plus Greek specialities. Leave
room for the delicious home-made desserts.
✉ Kremásti Square, Corfu Town ☎ 26610-44761 🕐 Lunch and dinner.
Closed Sun

Ways to be a local

Take time over your taverna meals. Talk a great deal, without inhibitions. Be demonstrative. Reservations for town restaurants and for the more sophisticated and popular resort restaurants are advisable in high season, but for most beach-side and village tavernas, phoning in advance is often irrelevant. The owners pack you in with gusto and good humour. If a taverna is full, extra tables and chairs may simply be added to garden, yard or village square. Squeeze in, tuck in, and enjoy it...

Buy worry beads, known as *kombologi*. (Unfortunately bead-worrying is an entirely male habit, which is a worry in itself.)

Drink *Ellinikos kafes* (Greek coffee). Take small sips and top up with water. Alternatively, brace yourself for ouzo; potent, but very Greek. Never add water to the glass. Instead match ouzo and water, sip for sip.

Prise yourself off the sun-lounger (if the ouzo hasn't won) and head into the hills on foot, or visit one of Corfu's enchanting inland villages, such as Doukádes, Lefkímmi or Ágios Matthéos.

Go fishing off the Old Port quays. Use a small hook, a light line and bread paste for bait. If you catch anything, act as if nothing has happened, but casually wave the fish in the air for a second or two.

Enjoy *kafes frappe* (iced coffee) in the Liston of a morning. Haggle over the price – if you dare.

Wear sober clothing and visit at least one of Corfu's many historic country churches. The Greek Orthodox Church is the official Church on Corfu and is strongly represented, although with its history of Venetian and later British presence the island has always supported other denominations, too.

Look out for a local carnival or festival and merge with the crowd. Suspend any plans you may have made for the rest of the day; and the night for that matter.

Keep your head held high, with your eyes constantly swivelling to the right and to the left, and move very fast when negotiating pedestrian crossings in the bustling San Rocco Square area of Corfu Town.

Accept, of course, that you are not a local, but get close to the experience by appreciating and respecting the spirited and generous lifestyle of the Corfiots.

Good places to have lunch

Bougainvillea (€€)

A delightful position overlooking the Plateía Dimarcheío (Town Hall Square) in Corfu Town adds to the pleasing experience of this friendly restaurant that offers a range of Corfiot specialities at their best as well as tasty dishes from elsewhere in Greece.

✉ Town Hall Square, Corfu Town ☎ 26610-41607

Cavo Barbaro (€–€€)

Cheerful service and good traditional food at laid-back Avlaki Beach on the northeast coast. This is old-style Corfiot cooking at its best with fish and meat dishes and treats such as onion pie.

✉ Avlaki Beach ☎ 26630-81905

Elisabeth's (€)

This unpretentious taverna at the heart of the endearing village of Doukádes is something of a Corfiot institution. Enjoy tasty soups and *pastitsada* and unfussy *choriatiki* (Greek salad).

✉ Main street,
Doukádes
☎ 26630-41728

En Plo (€€)

Marvellous venue with views across the sea to the Old Fortress. Stylish lunch snacks, salads, *moussaká* and a pricier selection of meat or fish *mezes*.

✉ St Nikolas Gate, Faliraki, Corfu Town
☎ 26610-81813

La Famiglia (€–€€)

Full-blooded Italian café-restaurant. Imaginative snacks and light meals on a busy, colourful street. Linguine with *vongole* (musssels); lasagne, including a vegetarian version; canelloni; *polenta con pancetta*. Imaginative desserts.

✉ 30 Maniarizi Arlioti Street, Corfu Town ☎ 26610-30270

Gallini (€€)

Highly popular waterfront taverna. Good steaks, *kheftiko* and other Greek dishes.

✉ Ágios Stéfanos ☎ 26630-81492

Gorgona (€€–€€€)

You won't get *gorgona* (mermaid) on a platter at this terrific fish taverna, but the great selection of fresh fish and seafood and the palette of sauces is unbeatable.

✉ Main Street, Gouviá ☎ 26610-90261

Kafesas (€€)

A popular fish taverna above the beach in southwest Corfu. Delicious fish *mezes*.

✉ Ágios Geórgios (southwest) ☎ 26620-51196

O Paxinos (€€)

Cheerful, immaculate, family-run taverna at the heart of old Benítses offers traditional Corfiot casserole dishes and locally caught fish as well as delicious *mezes* and lunchtime delights.

✉ Harbour Square, Benítses ☎ 26610-72339

Sea Breeze (€€)

Popular taverna in a lovely location with terraces overlooking the sea. Good Corfiot cuisine and Greek party nights.

✉ Ágios Górdis ☎ 26610-53214

Activities

Basketball: in every resort, there will be a basketball practice area. There are basketball courts at the New Port in Corfu Town.

Cricket: a famous legacy of the Victorian British Protectorate. Matches are traditionally played on summer afternoons at the north end of the Esplanade, in front of the Liston.
Kerkyra Cricket Committee ☎ 26610-47754

Diving: outstanding venues. Contact a local diving club or school for safety information. The Greek authorities are extremely sensitive about security at military installations on the island. The use of underwater cameras is forbidden by law unless prior permission is obtained from port authorities. Divers are strongly advised not to dive in working harbours or at busy anchorages.
Calypso Diving Centre ✉ Ágios Górdis ☎ 26610-53101;
www.divingcorfu.com
Corfu Divers ✉ Kassiopi ☎ 26630-29226; www.corfudivers.com
Corcyra Diving Centre ✉ Paleokastritsa ☎ 26630-41604;
www.corfuscubadiving.com

Golf: Corfu's only golf club has an 18-hole course described by *Encyclopedia of Golf* as 'one of the greatest courses in Europe'.
✉ Rópa Valley, Érmones ☎ 26610-94220 ✋ Expensive

Horse-back riding: either of the following offer great trails.
Rópa Valley Riding Stables ✉ Érmones ☎ (26610) 94220 ✋ Moderate
Trailriders for rides through the delightful Áno Korakiána area.
✉ Áno Korakiána ☎ 26630-23090/22503 ✋ Moderate

Mountain biking: rentals, cycling trips and holidays available.
Moraïtika Bike Hire ✉ At southern exit of Moraïtika
The Mountain Bike Shop ✉ Main street, Dassiá ☎ Summer 26610-93344. Also has a branch at Grecotel Dafníla Bay Thalosso Hotel, Dassía
Mountain Mania Bike Hire ✉ Main street south, Sidári ☎ 26630-95555

Sailing: the Ionian Sea is one of the most amenable areas of the Mediterranean for sailors. The Gouviá Marina has very good berthing facilities for those with their own vessels.
Gouviá Marina ☎ 26610-91475/91376; **Corfu Yachting** ✉ 12 Dorpfeld Street ☎ 26610-99470; www.corfu yacthing.com
Ionian Marine Holidays ✉ 16 Eth Antistasseos Street ☎ 26610-32273; www.ionian marine.co.uk

Tennis: several luxury and A-class hotels have their own tennis courts which may be available to non-residents.
Corfu Tennis Club ✉ 4 Romanou Street/Vraila Street, Corfu Town
☎ 26610-37021 ⏰ The courts are available to non-members 8am to midday

Water sports: water-sports facilities include pedaloes, canoes, banana boats, ringos, jet-ski trips and paragliding. Parents, of early teens especially, should be very careful that youngsters do not rent jet-skis by themselves. Some operators have been known to be lax about imposing age-limit restrictions and about checking whether or not people have been drinking.

Windsurfing: there are windsurfing centres at the following resorts: Ágios Geórgios (Northwest), Ágios Geórgios (Southwest), Ágios Górdis, Ágios Stéfanos (Northwest), Aryllas, Avlaki Beach, Érmones, Glyfáda, Kávos, Moraïtika and Sidári.

a walk

through the Campiello

A short stroll through the oldest part of Corfu Town, visiting St Spyrídon's Church and the Byzantine Museum. Start at St Spyrídon's Square, off Theotoki Nikiforou, where the Paper Money Museum can be visited.

Leave the square by its far left-hand corner to reach the Church of St Spyrídon (➤ 38–39). Go left at the church door and down Kalogeretou beneath a vaulted archway. At the junction, go right along Filarmonikis.

Filarmonikis, as the name suggests, is where Corfu Town's Philharmonic Societies have their rehearsal rooms.

Continue ahead up steps into Plateía Ag Elenis, with its big central palm tree. Leave the square by its far left-hand corner and then cross a smaller square. Pass a supermarket, then turn left into Plateía Taxiarchón.

On the right is the 16th-century Church of Christ Pandocrator. It has a fine doorway and a sculpted angel on the gable.

Go through the square and go left and down three steps (ramp alongside) to pass through a narrow alleyway. Turn right up the next alleyway and climb steps into Plateía Kremasti (Kremasti Square) to the Venetian Well and the Church of the Virgin Kremasti.

The well-head at the centre of the square is a survivor from the medieval period.

Leave the square by the far corner of the church, then turn left and then right into a square with a huge central palm tree. Keep to the left of the tree and go along a lane past a bell-tower. At the T-junction, go left, then, after a few metres, go left again and continue to the Byzantine Museum (▶ 90). Go right down steps to Arseniou. Turn right, follow the seafront road to where a gate gives access to the arched gate of St George, and continue to the Esplanade.

Distance 2km (1.2 miles)
Time 1.5 hours, if Paper Money Museum, churches, and Byzantine Museum are visited
Start point St Spyrídon's Square
✚ Kérkyra 3e
End point Spianáda (Esplanade)
✚ Kérkyra 3e
Lunch Christa's Crêperie (€)
✉ Sophocleous Dousmani
☎ 26610-40227

Museums, art galleries and exhibitions

Archaeological Museum
See pages 50–51.

Art Café Gallery
Small gallery staging exhibitions by Corfiot and contemporary artists and craftspeople.
🖂 Palace of St Michael and St George, East Wing, Esplanade, Corfu Town
🕓 Daily 11–2, 6–9

Byzantine Museum
The Church of Panagia Antivouniotissa (Church of the Blessed Virgin) houses an outstanding collection of Byzantine art (➤ 90).
🖂 Arseniou (Mourayia) ☎ 26610-38313
🕓 Tue–Sun 8.30–3 ❓ Exhibits generally labelled in English as well as Greek

Castello Art Gallery
This modern complex houses interesting works of art on loan from the Greek National Art Gallery.
🖂 Kato Korakiana ☎ 26610-72227
🕓 Wed–Mon 9–4 (also Wed and Fri 5–9)

Folklore Museum of Central Corfu
Part of the building is a reconstruction of a 19th-century village house with furnishings and utensils. Exhibits include farming tools, musical instruments and traditional costumes (➤ 182).
🖂 Sinarades ☎ 26610-54962 🕓 All year Tue–Sun 9.30–2.30. Opening hours are flexible
✋ Inexpensive

Kapodistrias Museum

Memorabilia of John Capodistrias, the first president of a united Greece.

✉ Koukoritsa, near Evropoúli village, 5km (3 miles) west of Corfu Town ☎ 26610-39528 ⏱ 11–1 Wed and Sat

Municipal Art Gallery

Works in this gallery in the east wing of the Palace of St Michael and St George are mainly by 19th- and 20th-century Corfiot painters and sculptors, but there are also medieval paintings (➤ 86–87).

✉ Paláti tou Agíou Michaíl tou Georgíou (Palace of St Michael and St George, East Wing) ☎ 26610-39553 ⏱ Tue–Sat 8.30–3, Sun 9.30–2.30

Municipal Theatre of Corfu

Art exhibitions held in the foyer.

✉ G Theotoki ☎ 26610-33598

Museum of Asiatic Art

Housed in the Palace of St Michael and St George, the museum is a remarkable collection of Sino-Japanese art and artefacts (➤ 97).

✉ Spianáda (Esplanade) ☎ 26610-38124 ⏱ Tue–Sun 8.30–3

Solomos Museum

Reconstruction of the house in which the poet Dionysios Solomos lived and which was destroyed by bombs during World War II.

✉ 3rd Parados, Arseniou ☎ 26610-30674 ⏱ Jun–Oct daily 9.30–2; Nov–May 9.30–1 ❓ Labels are in Greek

Places to take the children

Banana boats
Banana boats and ringos, which involve floats being towed behind speedboats, appeal to children and young people. Banana boats are generally a safe option, but ringo-riding is not suited to young children. Some beaches have ringo-riding for children (➤ 178–179).

Boat excursions
There are numerous boat excursions from the larger resorts. The Calypso Star, a glass-bottomed boat, runs trips round the island from the Old Port.

East-coast beaches
Beaches on Corfu's east coast are mainly shingle and often quite narrow. They are usually very safe for bathing and can become very crowded. Beach equipment and water sports are available at most coastal resorts. Best beaches for children include: Ágios Stéfanos (Northeast) (➤ 122–123), Astrakeri (➤ 141), Barmpáti (➤ 128), Dassiá (➤ 130–131), Gouviá (➤ 131), Kalámi (➤ 44–45), Messongí (➤ 178) and Moraïtika (➤ 178–179).

Festivals
Local festivals (➤ 24–25) are excellent entertainment for children on holiday (adults too).

Go-carting
There are circuits at **Kanoni:** Karto-Mania ☎ 26610-43545; **Sidári:** Sidári Go-Kart ☎ 26630-99076.

Off-road tracks
Cycling on Corfu's public roads is not advised for very young children or for those who are inexperienced.

There is a vast network of off-road tracks which can be enjoyed. The best areas are in the low-lying southern part of Corfu and northern coastal strip behind Sidári (➤ 138), Róda (➤ 138) and Acharávi (➤ 120).

North-coast beaches

Corfu's north-coast beaches are generally much longer than their east-coast counterparts and have more sand. They tend to be narrow, but do not shelve steeply into the sea. They may be affected in the afternoons by onshore winds. Best beaches for children include Acharávi, Róda and Sidári.

Water parks

Corfu's water-fun park, **Aqualand**, has a wide range of waterslides and other aquatic attractions.

✉ Ágios Ionnas (on Pélekas–Érmones road) ☎ 26610-58351/52963; www.aqualand-corfu.com 🚌 Blue bus 8 from San Rocco Square, Corfu Town to Aqualand 🕐 May–Jun, Sep–Oct daily 10–6; Jul–Aug daily 10–7

Also **Hydropolis** ✉ On main road, on Kassiopi side of Acharávi ☎ 26630-64700

Water slides

There are small water slides at Ágios Geórgios (➤ 150) (Northwest), Moraïtika (➤ 178–179) and Sidári (➤ 138).

West-coast beaches

Corfu's west-coast beaches are sandier than those on the east coast and they are often longer and wider. They are less accessible and may be affected by wind at times. Best beaches for children include Ágios Stéfanos (Northwest), Ágios Geórgios (Northwest) (➤ 150), Ágios Górdis (➤ 168–169) and Glyfáda (➤ 158).

Best beaches

Ágios Geórgios, northwest (➤ 150) and southwest (➤ 168), have long stretches of sandy beach, good for families.

Ágios Stéfanos (northwest) is good for families. Safe bathing, all types of beach equipment, water sports and trips (➤ 152).

Barmpáti (Barbati) has a long shingle beach, ideal for families and relatively quiet (➤ 128).

Diapondía Islands, if you have the time to get there, for a reasonable sense of isolation (➤ 154).

Glyfáda, one of the finest beaches on the west coast of Corfu, with a long stretch of golden sand, and water sports of every kind, including sailing and windsurfing (➤ 158).

Halikounas Beach, Lake Korissión, for open space and peace and quiet, provided you walk south until well clear of the crowds in the lake area during high season (➤ 48–49).

Myrtiótissa, for nature in the raw (➤ 159). Officially, nude bathing is illegal in Greece, although some beaches are now designated as 'naturist'. Bathing nude 'unofficially' is best done with discretion. The Corfiots are broadminded but many will be offended by full nudity, especially near centres of population or within sight of a church. Topless bathing by women is virtually the norm on all beaches, but you should respect the sensibilities of local people when off the beach and near religious institutions.

Sidári, for all the family, from the young to the young at heart. Good beaches include the large Megali Beach at the southern entrance to the resort and the smaller Canal d'Amour beaches below the sculpted sandstone cliffs of Sidári's north-facing coast. There is shallow water and safe bathing here, with every beachside facility to hand; water sports in plenty, a big water slide, go-carts, and numerous restaurants, tavernas, bars and clubs (➤ 138–139).

Ýpsos (Ipsos); crowded, but handy for bars, clubs and tavernas (➤ 140).

Places to stay

Akrotiri Beach (€€–€€€)
This comfortable place has a superb location on the neck of a wooded peninsula overlooking the pebbled beach. Plenty of amenities available, including a pool, tennis and water sports.
✉ Overlooking the main bay, Paleokastritsa ☎ 26630-41237; www.akrotiri-beach.com 🕓 Apr–Oct

Bounias Apartments/Villa Alexandra (€–€€)
There's unbeatable value and quality at these lovely rooms and peaceful apartments, within minutes of Avlaki Beach and about 2km (1.2 miles) from Kassiópi.
✉ Kassiópi ☎ 26630-81183/26610-24333 🕓 Apr–Oct

Cavalieri (€€€)
In a beautifully reconstructed Venetian building at the quiet end of the Esplanade. Rooms are quite small, but pleasant. The rooftop bar, open to non-residents, is an experience in itself.
✉ 4 Kapodistriou, Corfu Town ☎ 26610-39041/39336; www.cavalieri-hotel.com 🕓 All year

Corfu Palace (€€€)
Top luxury hotel on seafront overlooking Garitsa Bay. Beautiful gardens, sun terraces, outdoor and indoor pools and a children's pool. *Haute cuisine* restaurant and in-house entertainment.
✉ 2 Leoforos Dimokratias, Corfu Town ☎ 26610-39485/39487; www.corfupalace.com 🕓 All year

Golden Fox (€€)
These fine apartments adjoin the Golden Fox restaurant. Terrific views from front rooms; discount on food at the restaurant.
✉ Lákones ☎ 26630-49101/2; www.corfugoldenfox.com 🕓 Apr–Oct

Grecotel Corfu Imperial (€€€)
Luxury-class hotel on peninsula, with sea views, set amid

landscaped gardens. Large swimming pool, tennis courts, beauty salon, restaurants, bars and access to private beaches.

✉ Komméno–Gouviá, Cape Komméno

☎ 26610-88400; www.grecotel.gr 🕔 Apr–Oct

Hotel Konstantinoupolis (€€)

This fine old building at the heart of the Old Port has had its rooms nicely renovated. Friendly and comfortable.

✉ 11 K Zavitsianoy Street, Corfu Town ☎ 26610-48716/8; www.konstantinoupolis.com.gr 🕔 All year

Nissaki Beach Hotel (€€–€€€)

A luxury hotel in a prime coastal position. Facilities include tennis courts, swimming pool; even crazy golf. Exclusive beach area below has water sports and amenities, plus beachside taverna.

✉ In own grounds, Nissaki ☎ 26630-91232/91233 🕔 Apr–Oct

San Giorgio Rooms (€)

Between the New Port and Gáïos, minutes from the town centre, these fine rooms and self-catering studios have great views.

✉ New Port/Gáïos, Paxos ☎ 26620-32223 🕔 May–Oct

Villa de Loulia (€€€)

For rare style this is the place to head for in the less crowded northwest. Elegant, imaginative interiors incorporate old-style Corfu architecture and decoration that reflect the building's early 19th-century heritage. There's a large pool; just right for the exclusive nine rooms.

✉ Perouládes ☎ 26630-95394 🕔 May–Oct

Best souvenirs

When buying souvenirs remember Greece takes the middle ground between the Western culture of fixed-price shopping and Eastern bargaining, or 'haggling'. Greeks love a good haggle and so should you. Although fixed-priced shopping is the norm, especially in Corfu Town, where brand-name and speciality shops predominate, you may still get a flavour of bargaining at local markets. Try also the side-street shops bedecked with clothes, rugs and general goods and the roadside stands of places such as Makrádes (➤ 158) on the northwest coast. It is only acceptable to haggle over non-perishable goods.

Lace from Kassiópi: try **Agatha's Lace,** a centre of Corfu lace-making, with a good selection of handmade lace goods and rugs.
✉ Main Street ☎ 26630-81315

Kumquat liqueur: this is a famous Corfiot liqueur, distilled from the tiny kumquat, a citrus fruit that looks like a miniature orange. The kumquat is native to South East Asia and was introduced to

Corfu in the 1860s. The standard kumquat drink is bright orange, the colour being derived from the rind; it is very sweet. There is a colourless distillation of kumquat juice which is far more potent and adventurous and can be identified by the 'twig' with attached crystals that floats inside the bottle. All manner of other drinks, candies, and sweets are produced using kumquats.

A subtle sun-tan: guard against sunburn and sunstroke. A holiday can be ruined in the first few days from too much exposure to the sun. Take precautions by using reputable sun-screening creams and by rationing your sunbathing. Be very careful not to expose young children to the sun for long periods.

A small bottle of ouzo: impress (or destroy) the taste buds of your friends back home. You'll find a selection of wines, spirits and liqueurs on sale at **Costas Thimis** in Corfu Town.
✉ N Theotoki ☎ 26610-44070

Olive-wood carving: *Elia*, or the phonetic 'elea', means olive or olive tree in Greek, and at **Elea** in Acharávi everything, including the shop itself, is made of olive wood.
✉ Main street, in centre

Worry beads *(kombologi)*
See page 60.

Bottle of virgin olive oil: the finest virgin olive oil can be bought in delicatessens.

Leather bag, or shepherd's woven satchel: the majority of resorts on Corfu have leather-goods' shops and other gift shops. Most close down for the winter.

Baklava (syrup cakes), *kataifi* (honey cakes) and *mandolato* (nougat): there are many mouth-watering *zaharoplastios*, shops that specialize in cakes, pastries and sweets, so indulge yourself.

Gold or silver jewellery: gold and silver shops have proliferated in Corfu in recent years and offer quite good bargains compared with mainstream European outlets.

Exploring

Corfu has golden sandy beaches, water sports of every kind, choice places to eat and an abundance of nightlife; but there is also a wealth of woodland, mountains and undeveloped coast that provide havens of peace and quiet to explore. The island is steeped in history: in ancient times it was known variously as Scheria and as Drepane, the word for 'sickle', a reference that is thought to derive from the island's long, curved shape. By the medieval period the name Corfu was established. There are several explanations of this name. It is said to derive from the Greek word *koryphai*, meaning 'summit' or 'twin peaks', a possible reference to the two rocky outcrops on which the Old Fortress of Corfu Town is built. Another suggestion is that the Norman invaders of the 12th century named their anchorages north of modern Corfu Town *Corfi*, the Greek plural version of the Latin word for bay, *golfo*.

Kérkyra (Corfu Town)

The original settlement of Corfu Town was on the southern tip of the Kanóni Peninsula to the south of the present town. Then, in the 6th century, a more dangerous world emerged and the town's citizens, exhausted from savage barbarian raids, moved to the small, twin-peaked peninsula where the Old Fortress now stands. Gradually a town developed

outside the fortress, but within its own defensive walls. Later expansion saw Corfu Town spread to the south and west to form an outer shell of suburbs that evolved into the district surrounding San Rocco Square.

The magic of Corfu Town is at its most potent where new and old meet at M Theotoki Square. Here, you step from the bustle of a modern Greek town into the arcaded, smoothly paved streets of medieval times, your way signposted by Greek street names, Greek churches, and by a sense of more variety to come. Soon, you reach the famous Esplanade, its western edge framed by the arcaded Liston. At its northern edge is the Palace of St Michael and St George, symbol of British neoclassicism. Beyond all this, to the east, Byzantine Greece is represented, in spirit, by the Old Fortress, whose Venetian walls stand on Corinthian foundations.
www.gnto.gr ✚ 32S

ÁGIOS IÁSONAS KAI SOSIPÁTROS (CHURCH OF ST JASON AND ST SOSIPATER)

Corfu's sole example of 10th- to early 11th-century Byzantine architecture stands in a rather anonymous corner of Anemomylos, a suburb on the southern edge of Corfu Town. Jason and Sosipater were bishops of Tarsus and Iconium respectively, who brought Christianity to Corfu during the first century when the island was under Roman rule. They are said to have been martyred for it. The church is of typical Byzantine design, built in the shape of a cross, with a handsome central dome crowning an octagonal drum. Beams of sunlight passing through the stained glass of the dome create luminous pools of colour. There are a number of fine icons, and a mix of styles and periods. There is an 18th-century iconostasis, and the plain marble columns that help to support the dome are believed to originate from a classical temple of ancient Palaiopolis (➤ 96).

✚ *Kérkyra 3a* ✉ Iásonas kai Sosipátros (Jason and Sosipater Street) 🕎 Free; donations welcome 🍴 Cafés, tavernas (€) in Nafsikas and Dimokratias 🚌 2 Kanóni. Blue bus from San Rocco Square. Get off at Nafsikas Street 🔗 Ruined Basilica of Palaiopolis (➤ 96) ❓ Sober clothing should be worn. Ask for key at adjacent house if church is locked

ÁGIOS SPYRÍDONAS

See pages 38–39.

ANAGNOSTIKÍ ETAIRÍA KERKYRAS (CORFU READING SOCIETY)

This venerable society was founded in 1836 by a group of young Corfiot intellectuals, giving it a claim to being the oldest cultural institution in modern Greece. The Society's premises are in a handsome Venetian building at the south end of Arseniou near the Palace of St Michael and St George. Its arcaded façade incorporates an outside staircase and an upper verandah. At street level, a small relief of an owl, symbol of wisdom, strikes a charming and witty note.

The interior of the building has the comfortable, well-worn atmosphere of all good libraries; the walls are hung with paintings and prints.

There is an impressive collection of Ionian-related books, manuscripts, periodicals, engravings, maps and other material by Greek and foreign authors. Researchers and interested visitors are welcomed with great courtesy.

➕ *Kérkyra 3f* ✉ 120 Kapodistriou Street ⏰ Mon–Sat 9.15–1.45
✋ Free 🍴 En Plo (€€) ↔ Palace of St Michael and St George (▶ 97)
❓ The library and the reading room are open to the public

ANGLIKÓ NEKROTAFEÍO (BRITISH CEMETERY)

There is nothing gloomy about a visit to this tree-shaded and flower-filled oasis of peace and quiet. More English garden than burial plot, it was established during the period of the British Protectorate and contains the graves of soldiers who died in service during the 19th and 20th centuries. Civilians are buried here, too.

The cemetery, under the care of the British War Graves Commission, owes much of its charm to the dedication of long-serving caretaker, George Psailas, who was born in the peaceful little guardian house and who, over many years, has tended the cemetery's green spaces with great devotion.

In spring the cemetery is awash with the colour of shrubs and flowers, most notably a remarkable number of orchids, which are allowed to bloom and seed before the grass-cutting begins.

✚ *Kérkyra 1c* ✉ Kolokotroní (off Mitropolitou Methodiou) 🕓 All day

🍴 Cafés and restaurants (€–€€) in nearby Mitropolitou Methodiou

CAMPIELLO (OLD CORFU TOWN)

See pages 42–43.

DIMOTIKÍ PINAKOTHÍKI (MUNICIPAL ART GALLERY)

This gallery was opened in 1995 in the east wing of the Palace of
St Michael and St George (► 97). The exhibition rooms are a
pleasure in themselves, and the approach, through a tree-shaded
garden and past the Art Café and Bar, is charming. The works in
the gallery are mainly by 19th- and 20th-century Corfiot painters
and sculptors, but there are also medieval paintings including the
Decapitation of John The Baptist by Michael Damaskinos. Corfiot
painters include Charalambos Pachis, whose *The Assassination of
Capodistrias* is a touch melodramatic, but compelling. The French-
influenced painting of the Liston, *Night in Corfu* (1913), by George
Samartzis, has a happy relevance for holidaymakers. Modern
works by the engraver Nikolaos Ventouras, and later abstract

paintings by Aglaia Papa, are also on display. Next to the café-bar there is another smaller gallery, which stages various exhibitions.

➕ *Kérkyra 3f* ✉ Paláti tou Agíou Michaíl tou Georgíou (Palace of St Michael and St George, East Wing) ☎ 26610-39553 🕐 Tue–Sat 8.30–3, Sun 9.30–2.30 ✋ Moderate 🍽 Art Gallery Café (€€), behind the palace 🔄 Palace of St Michael and St George (➤ 97), Old Fortress (➤ 94–95)

KANÓNI

See pages 46–47.

MITRÓPOLI (CATHEDRAL)

Corfu's Orthodox cathedral, the Cathedral of Panagia Spiliotissa (Madonna of the Grotto), stands at the top of a flight of steps set back from the Old Port Square. The 16th-century building, which did not become a cathedral until 1841, is dedicated to St Theodora Augusta, whose mummified remains were brought to Corfu at the same time as those of the more celebrated St Spyrídon. They lie in a silver casket in the cathedral.

The interior of the cathedral is lined with wooden panelling. There is a white iconostasis with a broken pediment, and the numerous icons include a beautiful image of the Archangel Michael and one of the Virgin.

➕ *Kérkyra 2f* ✉ Plateía Konstantinou, off Old Port Square 🕐 Daily 9–2. Avoid casual visits during services ✋ Free, donations welcome 🍽 Cafés, restaurants (€–€€) in Old Port Square 🔄 Old Port Square (➤ 98) ❓ Sober clothing should be worn. Ceremony on first Sunday of Lent when relics of St Theodora are carried around town

MON REPOS

The elegant villa of Mon Repos was built on a choice site on the Kanóni Peninsula in 1831 for the British High Commissioner, Sir Frederick Adam. Its style is neoclassical, with a nod to the Byzantine in its rotunda. The British ceded Mon Repos to King George I of Greece on their withdrawal from Corfu in 1864. Prince Philip, Duke of Edinburgh, was born here in 1921.

The house had a chequered history in subsequent years and lay neglected as legal disputes dragged on between the former King Constantine of Greece and the Municipality of Corfu. The latter has restored the property, which is now fully open to the public and incorporates the Museum of Palaiópolis. Exhibits include displays on ancient Kérkyra.

At the southern end of the grounds are the impressive ruins of a Doric temple of about 500BC. The only parking available is near the entrance gate and is very limited. An on-site café is planned, but you are advised to bring water with you.

➕ *Kérkyra 4a (off map)* ✉ Nafsikas, Anemomylos ☎ 26610-41369
🕐 House: Tue–Sun 8.30–3. Park: daily 8.30–7 ✋ Grounds free, museum moderate 🍴 Café (€), tavernas (€–€€) in nearby Garítsa 🚌 2 Kanóni. Blue bus from San Rocco Square ↔ Christian Basilica of Palaiopolis (➤ 96)

MOUSEÍO ARCHAIOLOGIKÓ (ARCHAEOLOGICAL MUSEUM)

See pages 50–51.

MOUSEÍO SOLOMOÚ (SOLOMOS MUSEUM)

The poet Dionysios Solomos (1798–1857) was born on the island of Zakynthos but spent his later life on Corfu. He championed the

modern Greek language, and in 1863 the first two stanzas of his
1822 poem, 'Hymn to Liberty', were set to music by his friend, the
composer Nicholas Mantzaros. The combined work became the
Greek national anthem. The museum is a reconstruction of the
house in which Solomos lived and which was destroyed during
World War II. The atmosphere alone is rewarding.

✚ *Kérkyra 2f* ✉ 3rd Parados, Arseniou ☎ 26610-30674 🕐 Jun–Oct
Mon–Fri 9.30–2; Nov–May Mon–Fri 9.30–1 ✋ Moderate 🍴 Cafés,
restaurants (€–€€) in Old Port Square ↔ Byzantine Museum (▶ 90)
❓ Labels in Greek only. No photography

MOUSEÍO VIZANTINÓ (BYZANTINE MUSEUM)

The Church of Panagia Antivouniotissa (Church of the Blessed Virgin), which houses this outstanding collection of Byzantine art, dates from the 16th century. There are about 90 icons on display, most from the 13th to the 17th centuries and depicting individual saints and biblical scenes. There is also outstanding work by the Cretan painters Emanuel Tzanes and Michael Damaskinos, among others. The plain outside walls of the church mask a beautiful interior of enclosed arcades surrounding a central nave with a coffered and decorated ceiling, painted walls and gilded woodwork.

✚ *Kérkyra 3f* ✉ Arseniou (Mourayia) ☎ 26610-38313 🕐 Tue–Sun 8.30–3 ✋ Moderate 🍴 Cafés, restaurants (€–€€) in Old Port Square, Faliraki (€€) ↔ Solomos Museum (➤ 88–89) ❓ Exhibits generally in English and Greek. No flash photography

NÉO FROÚRIO (NEW FORTRESS)

The New Fortress is 'new' only in the sense that it was started in 1572, a mere 15 years after the Venetians began rebuilding the Old Fortress. The massive outerworks of this 'Néo Froúrio' were built by the Venetians, but the buildings that survive within the walls, a mass of tunnels, vaulted chambers and stairways, were added by the British. On its eastern side are two entrances: an unused one in Solomou Square; the other, in New Fortress Square, is the military gate, used by the resident naval authorities. Public entrance is via the steep stone steps that lead up from the far end of the square past the Roman Catholic Church of Tenedos. There are fine views from the bastions and at the top a café/bar, exhibition centre and museum of ceramics (not always open).

✚ *Kérkyra 1f* ✉ Solomos Street, off Spilia Square or New Fortress Square ☎ 26610-27477 🕐 May–Oct daily 9–9 ✋ Moderate 🍴 Café (€), tavernas (€–€€) in nearby Old Port Square ↔ Old Port (➤ 98)

a walk into the past

A walk through the historic southern part of Corfu Town.

Start at the Peristýlio Maitland (Maitland Rotunda, ➤ 106). Continue south on Dimokratias, alongside the sea, to the small harbour at Anemomylos. Here, on the seaward point, beyond the Nautilus Café, is a restored windmill. Pass the café and bear right along the edge of the sea until opposite Hotel Mon Repos. Cross the road, with care, then go down the lane to the left of the hotel. Pass Ágios lásonas kai Sosipátros (the Church of St Jason and St Sosipater, ➤ 83) on the left.

Turn first right just past the church. Reach a tree-shaded walkway (toilets) and turn left. At a road junction cross

left, with care, and follow the continuation walkway to reach Oveliskos Ntalklas (the Douglas Obelisk). Cross left to the British Consulate.

The obelisk commemorates General Sir Howard Douglas, the 4th British High Commissioner, an able administrator.

Go up the street to the left of the consulate. At a junction go straight across and past railings to reach Stíli tou Menekráti (the Tomb of Menekrates).

This 6th-century cenotaph celebrates Menekrates, a representative of ancient Corcyra.

Continue along Kyprou (Cyprus) Street for about 100m (110yds), then make a sharp U-turn to the right on to a road rising through trees. Continue until you reach a T-junction by the walls of Corfu Prison. Turn left and follow the walls round past the prison's main gate. Bear left, and then right down Kolokotroni Street to Angliko Nekrotafeio (the British Cemetery, ➤ 84–85). Continue on to a busy junction with Mitropolitou Methodiou. Turn right and then continue to San Rocco Square.

Distance 5km (3 miles)
Time 1.5 hours
Start point Maitland Rotunda
End point San Rocco Square
Lunch Cafés and tavernas ✉ Mitr Athanassiou (€)

NÉO LIMANI (NEW PORT)

The area of the New Port is neither scenic nor tourist-oriented, but it is a lively place, full of everyday activities and the rattle and hum of seagoing vessels. Boats, large and small, throng the working harbour, while the big mainland and island ferries come and go along the quays further north. The busy seafront road is lined with ships' chandlers, marine suppliers and workshops, as well as travel agencies and car-rental firms. At the western end is the old and down-to-earth district of Mandouki, with its cafés and tavernas.

✚ Kérkyra 1f (off map)
✉ Ethnikis Antistasseos
✋ Free 🍴 Cafés, tavernas
(€–€€) in nearby Mandouki
🚢 Main port for big ferries
🔄 Monastery of the Virgin
(► 105), Old Port (► 98)

PALAIÓ FROÚRIO (OLD FORTRESS)

The Palaió Froúrio (Paleo Froúrio) is a powerful visual symbol of town and island. The earliest known fortifications were Byzantine, established in the 6th century after the destruction of the old Corinthian city of Palaiopolis (► 96) by Goth raiders. The Venetians replaced and extended the walls in the 15th century and excavated the defensive moat, the Contrafossa, that now adds such a picturesque element to the scene. Further rebuilding took place between 1558 and 1588, and it is these fortifications that survive today.

The fortress is approached from the east side of the Esplanade. The right-hand guardhouse in the main gatehouse houses the Byzantine Collection of Corfu with mosaics and sculptures from the Basilica of Palaiopolis. There are fresco fragments from St Nicholas's church in Kato Korakiana. Across the bridge is the

Church of the Madonna of the Carmelites. The summit of the inner peak, the Castel a Terra (Landward Castle), with its little lighthouse, can be reached by a steep climb past a Venetian clock-tower. At 72m (236ft) high, the view over Corfu Town and inland to Mount Pandokrator (➤ 54–55) is spectacular.

There is a maze of tunnels, excavated by the Venetians, beneath the Old Fortress and the New Fortress. One tunnel is said to run beneath the sea to Vídos Island, which lies just offshore from the town. Vídos was strategically important to both attack on the town and, when fortified, to its defence.

✠ *Kérkyra 4e* ✉ Spianáda (Esplanade) ☎ 26610-48310 🕓 May–Oct daily 8.30–7; Nov–Apr daily 8.30–3 💷 Expensive 🍴 Café (€€) 🔁 Municipal Art Gallery (➤ 86–87), Palace of St Michael and St George (➤ 97), Esplanade (➤ 106)

PALAIOPOLIS (ANCIENT CITY OF CORCYRA)

Poignant relics of Palaiopolis (Paleopolis), the ancient city of
Corcyra, survive on the Kanóni Peninsula 5km (3 miles) south of
Corfu Town. One of the oldest ruins is the Tower of Nerandzicha, a
remnant of the city walls dating from the 5th century BC. Close by
are the impressive remains of the late 6th-century BC Temple of
Artemis, from which the Gorgon pediment, now housed in Corfu
Town's Archaeological Museum (➤ 50–51), was recovered.

On the road to Kanóni, opposite the gates to Mon Repos
(➤ 88), are the ruins of the 5th-century Christian Basilica of
Palaiopolis. Nearby are the ruins of Roman baths of about AD200.

✚ *Kérkyra 4a (off map)* or 32R ✉ Anemomylos ✋ Free 🍴 Cafés, tavernas
(€–€€) in nearby Garitsa 🚌 2 Kanóni. Blue bus from San Rocco Square
↔ Mon Repos (➤ 88)

PALÁTI TOU AGÍOU MICHAÍL TOU GEORGÍOU
(PALACE OF ST MICHAEL AND ST GEORGE)

Dominating the Plateía, the northern end of the Esplanade, the palace is the most striking relic of the 50-year British presence on Corfu. It was built between 1819 and 1824 during the service of Sir Thomas Maitland, the first High Commissioner, and was used as the official seat of the Protectorate. The palace is triumphantly neoclassical in style, with a passing nod to the Parthenon in its Doric portico. In the garden in front of the palace stands a statue of Sir Frederick Adam, second High Commissioner.

The interior is outstanding: the finest feature is the rotunda on the first floor, its domed ceiling painted in blue and gold, its walls punctuated with mahogany doors, niches and mirrored panels.

Several of the state rooms house the Museum of Asiatic Art, a remarkable collection of Sino-Japanese art and artefacts, including mosaics from the early Christian Basilica of Palaiopolis (opposite).

Chinese and Japanese exhibits make up the largest part of the collection but there are also objects from India, Tibet, Nepal, Korea and Thailand. Items include prehistoric bronzes, porcelain ware, woodcarvings, Noh theatre masks, Samurai armour and weapons and much more. The palace also houses the Municipal Art Gallery (➤ 86–87) and the Modern Art Museum.

✚ Kérkyra 3f ✉ Spianáda (Esplanade) ☎ 26610-30443
🕐 Tue–Sun 8.30–3 🚶 Moderate 🍴 Art Gallery Café (€€) 🔁 New Fortress (➤ 90), Old Fortress (➤ 94–95), Esplanade (➤ 106)

PALÉO LIMANI (OLD PORT)

There is an unassuming charm about the Old Port which reflects its historic role as a maritime and commercial centre. Old Port Square was once used for the town market, and local people still gather here to gossip and relax. The quays are used for car parking, but the inner square has been landscaped and is lined with some fine old buildings, including the Law Courts and the Constantinople Hotel. Lanes and alleyways lead temptingly into the old town from here.

Behind the Law Courts is a splendid medieval relic, the gate of the Venetian Granary, complete with a stone relief of the trireme, or rowing galley – the emblem of Old Corfu. The right-hand side of Old Port Square leads into Solomou Square and then into Spilia Square, or New Fortress Square, and so to the New Fortress; the district is still called Ovriaki from its time as the Jewish Quarter.

There are a number of cafés and tavernas in Old Port Square. From the square, Donzelot Street leads up to the area known as the Mourayia and into Arseniou Street. Here, you can see Venetian buildings, as well as the Solomos Museum and the Byzantine Museum.

✚ *Kérkyra 2f* ✉ Spilia ⑪ Cafés, tavernas (€–€€) 🚹 Free 🚢 Ferry port for Paxos and excursions 🔁 Cathedral of Panagia Spiliotissa (➤ 87), New Fortress (➤ 90), Solomos Museum (➤ 88–89), Byzantine Museum (➤ 90)

PLATEÍA AGÍOU SPYRÍDONA
(ST SPYRÍDON'S SQUARE)

This attractive Italianate square lies at the heart of Corfu Town. Its official name is Plateía Iroon Kypriakou Agonos, the Square of the Heroes of the Cypriot Struggle, but the nearby Church of St Spyrídon has given it the more manageable name of St Spyrídon's Square, or the Saint's Square. Two other churches stand nearby. The Church of the Virgin of Strangers, which dates from the 1680s, became the favoured church of exiled Greeks from mainland Epirus fleeing from their Turkish oppressors. The interior of the church is particularly rich in icons and frescoes. The other church is that of St John the Baptist, or St John at the Cisterns, named after the rainwater tanks that once lay beneath the square. On the western side of the square is the handsome classical façade of the 19th-century Ionian Bank.

✚ *Kérkyra 3e* 🍽 Café Plakada (€€) ↔ Church of St Spyrídon (➤ 38–39)

an excursion to Paxoí and Antipaxoí

PAXOÍ (PAXOS)

Paxoí (Paxos) lies 48km (30 miles) to the south of Corfu Town, just 11km (7 miles) south of Ákrotírio Asprókavos, and is a popular destination for day excursions from Corfu. It is decidedly up-market, thanks to the large number of visiting yacht crews and to Paxos devotees with a proprietorial air. Prices tend to be above the average for the Ionian as a whole, due in part to the high cost of imports.

The island, 11km (7 miles) long and 5km (3 miles) wide, is swathed in olive trees, pines and cypresses, giving the hilly interior a deceptively rounded look. It is a delightful place, where life is measured at a much slower pace than on Corfu. Dusty tracks wind through the olive groves to small settlements or to remote coves and pebble beaches – although Paxos is not a beach-lover's paradise.

The south and west coasts are particularly spectacular, with steep cliffs, huge, cathedral-like sea caves and wind-sculpted rock formations, such as the stupendous pinnacle of Tripitos, linked by an arch to the south coast. The limestone of the cliffs glows pink and ochre in the setting sun.

The Venetians oversaw the 15th-century transformation of Paxos into one enormous olive grove, and the Paxíots created an almost formal landscape of terraces and drystone walling that survives today. The Venetian influence is seen also in the buildings of the island's principal port, Gáïos, and in tiny hamlets and numerous scattered ruins. Offshore from Gáïos is the tree-covered island of St Nicholas, complete with its ruins of a 15th-century Venetian fortress. The smaller Panagia Islet has an old church and a lighthouse.

The two other main settlements are Lákka at the northern tip of the island, and Longós, on the east coast,

midway between Gáïos and Lákka. Buses operate
between all three, but exploring the island on foot is a
rewarding option, although you need more than a day visit
to get the best from this Ionian jewel.

ANTIPAXOÍ (ANTIPAXOS)

Antipaxos is only a few kilometres from Paxos and can
be reached from Gáïos by fast ferry boat. A mere 3sq km
(1sq mile) in size, the island is a complex of tracks and
paths through olive- and vine-growing country, a place
where some kind of solitude can be found even at the
height of summer. The east-coast beaches at Vrika,
Mesovrika and Voutoumi are attractive, although they tend
to become crowded with day visitors.

Getting there

Ferries operate to Paxos from Corfu Town and there are
cruise boats from Kávos. It is essential to make enquiries
at several ferry agencies because of a complex and often
changing ferry system. There is a seaplane service run by
AirSea Lines that operates between Gouviá, Corfu and
Paxos (➤ 26 and 28).

PLATEÍA DEMARCHÍOU (TOWN HALL SQUARE)

Known officially as Plateía Demarchíou, this attractive central square, where there are several craft shops and pâtisseries, descends in a series of paved terraces from south to north. At the centre stands a bust of Iakovos Polylas (1825–93), friend of the poet Dionysios Solomos, and himself a distinguished writer and translator. Guilford Street, named after Frederick North, fifth Earl of Guilford, leads into the square. Guilford was a genial eccentric and enthusiastic Grecophile, who converted to Greek Orthodoxy and brought to fruition John Capodistrias's dream of an Ionian Academy, the first university in modern Greece. Count John Capodistrias (Ioannis Kapodistrias; 1776–1831) was a celebrated Corfiot who, in 1827, became the first President of Independent Greece. In 1831 his career was cut short when he was assassinated at Náfplio in the Peloponnese by critics of his political programme. Born in Corfu in 1776, Capodistrias practised as a doctor, and then entered island politics. During the French occupation of Corfu he left the island and joined the Russian foreign service. In 1822 he retired and devoted himself to the cause of Greek independence. Capodistrias is buried in Moní Platytéras (the Monastery of Platitéra) in Corfu Town. A small museum in Evropoúli, to the west of the town, celebrates his life.

The focus of the square is Corfu Town Hall, an intriguing building that has undergone a number of transformations since its origins in the late 17th century as an open arcade, the Loggia dei Nobili, a meeting place of the Venetian hierarchy. It was subsequently converted to a theatre, and a second floor was added when it became the Town Hall in

1903. On the east wall is a spectacular marble relief depicting Francesco Morosini – Venetian Admiral (later Doge of Venice), Hammer of the Turks in the Peloponnese, and incidental demolisher of the Athenian Parthenon when he bombarded the Turkish-held Acropolis in 1687 (the Parthenon was the Turk's gunpowder store). Morosini glares threateningly at the handsome façade of the Roman Catholic Cathedral of St James and St Christopher diagonally opposite. The original St James's was a parish church of 1588 and became a cathedral in 1633. After much damage from bombing in 1943, the present building was restored.

✝ *Kérkyra 3e* ✋ Free 🍴 Bougainvillea (€–€€)

PLATEÍA G THEOTÓKI IOÁNNOU (SAN ROCCO SQUARE)

Corfu Town's commercial heart is as brash and traffic-bound as central Athens. But it does have a heart. The central plaza has seating, though a pause for quiet reflection is not an option, and busy shopping streets radiate from all corners. There are numerous hot-food shops and several street kiosks along the north side. The Blue Bus terminus is on the southeast side. Polihroni Konstanda Street leads off the west corner of San Rocco and, though heavy with traffic, is worth exploring for its arcaded walkways and food shops. Mitropolitou Methodiou Street leads southwest, and the attractive Alexandras Avenue, with a number

of pavement cafés, leads southeast. G Theotoki Street leads northeast into the old town past some wonderful shops, especially on its south side. Do not miss the morning market, reached up Gerasimou Markora Street on the north side of San Rocco Square.

✚ *Kérkyra 2d* 🍴 Cafés, restaurant (€–€€)

PLATITÉRA (MONASTERY OF THE VIRGIN)

Platitéra, meaning 'Wider than the Heavens', is an oasis of calm alongside Corfu Town's busy link road to the coast road north: traffic hurtles past the palm-filled little entrance courtyard and its tall, red-domed bell-tower. Although the original 18th-century convent was set on fire by the French in 1798 in response to a revolt against them by local people, it was soon rebuilt. There are very fine icons and paintings inside the church, although the poor light does not do them justice. The most dramatic are The *Day of Judgement*, by the 16th-century Cretan painter George Klotzas, and the *Allegory of Heavenly Jerusalem*, or, more pointedly, *The Damned and the Blessed*, by an unknown 16th-century artist. The latter brims with graphic symbols of wickedness. Behind the sanctuary is the tomb of Count John Capodistrias.

✚ *Kérkyra 1d (off map)* ✉ Andreadi
🕐 Daily 9–2 💰 Free, but donations welcomed 🍴 Cafés, tavernas (€–€€) in nearby Mandouki 🔄 New Port (➤ 94)
❓ Sober clothing should be worn

THE SPIANÁDA (ESPLANADE) AND THE LISTON

Corfu Town's Esplanade is one of the most charming urban open spaces in the Mediterranean. It owes its open nature to the Venetians, who cleared the medieval town that lay in front of the fortress. They ensured that the line of their buildings along the western edge incorporated straight alleyways to allow direct lines of fire from the Old Fortress. These buildings survive along Kapodistriou Street, but on the Plateía, the northern section of the Esplanade, the terrace of arcaded buildings known as the Liston was built by the French in the style of the Parisian rue de Rivoli. Today, with its stylish cafés and restaurants, the Liston is a focus for Corfu Town at play. In front of the Liston is the wide green space used for cricket matches.

The southern half of the Esplanade is landscaped and has an elegant bandstand where the town's brass bands perform on summer Sunday afternoons. At its far end is the Peristýlio Maitland (Maitland Rotunda), built in honour of Sir Thomas Maitland, the first High Commissioner during the early years of the British Protectorate.

🔢 *Kérkyra 3e* 🖐 Free 🍽 Café/restaurants (€€–€€€) on the Liston
🔄 Palace of St Michael and St George (➤ 97), Old Fortress (➤ 94–95)

HOTELS

Arcadion (€€€)
A 1960s building with a Venetian façade; fine position overlooking the end of the Liston and across the Esplanade to the Old Fortress. Great view from the front balconies. The Arcadion has had a thorough upgrade, as has its prices.

✉ 2 Vlasopoulou ☎ 26610-37670; www.arcadionhotel.com

Atlantis (€€)
Modern hotel at New Port, overlooking busy Xenofondos Stratigou Street. Several minutes' walk to town centre. Reasonable rooms. Very good restaurant and bar.

✉ 48 Xenofondos Stratigou ☎ 26610-35560; www.atlantis-hotel-corfu.com

Bella Venezia (€€)
Stylish hotel in refurbished classical mansion occupying the site of the original Bella Venezia destroyed in World War II. Charming gardens and a pavilion breakfast room and restaurant. In a quiet street midway between San Rocco Square and the Liston.

✉ 4 N Zambeli ☎ 26610-46500

Bretagne (€€)
Well-appointed modern hotel on the southern outskirts of Corfu Town. About 1.5km (1 mile) from the centre of town, but within walking distance of the airport.

✉ 27 Georgaki Ethnicou Stadiou, Garitsa ☎ 26610-30724/35690

Cavalieri (€€€)
See page 74.

Corfu Palace (€€€)
See page 74.

Hotel Konstantinoupolis (€€)
See page 75.

Palace Mon Repos (€€€)

This well-positioned Garitsa hotel has a restaurant and outdoor pool. It's about a 2km (1.2-mile) walk along the seafront into town.
✉ Anemomylos ☎ 26610-32783 ⊙ Apr–Oct

Phoenix (€)

The Phoenix is just over 1km (0.5 miles) from the centre of town on the street leading to the airport, which is about 0.75km (just under 0.5 miles) away. It has pleasant rooms and friendly service.
✉ 2 Chris. Smyrnis, Garitsa ☎ 26610-42290

KANÓNI
Corfu Divani Palace (€€€)

Modern luxury hotel with gardens, sun terrace and pool.
✉ 20 Nafsikas ☎ 26610-38996; www.divanis.gr ⊙ Apr–Oct

RESTAURANTS

Aegli (€€–€€€)

See page 58.

Arpi (€€)

Greek country cooking: start with *fasolata* (bean soup), then try the cockerel *pastitsada*, or *soopiess* (cuttlefish). Good Greek Cabernet.
✉ Panayioti Giotopoulou (off Town Hall Square) ☎ 26610-27715 ⊙ Lunch and dinner

Art Gallery Café (€€)

Pleasantly fashionable café-bar adjoining the Municipal Art Gallery. Good place to kick off an evening with drinks.
✉ Palace of St Michael and St George, East Wing, Esplanade ⊙ All day

Bougainvillea (€€)

See page 62.

Café Banca (€–€€)

Nicely placed just down from the busy San Rocco Square area, with a good selection of tasty snacks and range of drinks.

✉ 42b Alexandras Avenue (off San Rocco Square) ☎ 26610-43290
🕐 All day

Campiello Crêperie (€)

Good crêperie in quiet part of the Old Town. Large selection of crêpes and fine wines.

✉ 25 Petridou ☎ 26610-23517 🕐 Dinner

Chrisomallis (€)

See page 58.

Christa's Crêperie (€)

In great location just up from Filarmonikis. Delicious selection of crêpes and an intimate atmosphere.

✉ Sophocleous Dousmani ☎ 26610-40227 🕐 Lunch and dinner. Dinner only in winter

Crêperie Koukonára (€)

This busy streetside crêperie offers tasty take-aways.

✉ 7 Filarmonikis ☎ 26610-81737 🕐 All day

La Cucina (€€)

Italian restaurant specializing in home-made fresh pasta, served with seafood, smoked salmon or prosciutto; also excellent pizzas.

✉ 17 Guilford Street, Porta Remounda ☎ 26610-45029 🕐 Dinner

En Plo (€€)

See page 62.

La Famiglia (€–€€)

See page 63.

Il Giardino (€€€)

Classy Italian restaurant offering Tuscan cuisine and fine wines.

✉ 4b Vraila. Opposite the Archaeological Museum ☎ 26610-30723
🕐 Dinner

Kochlias (€€)

Liston bar-café. Variety of coffees, fresh fruit juices, ouzo, wines, beers, *mezes*, sandwiches and ice-cream.

✉ The Liston ☎ 26610-28188 🕐 All day

Mouragio (€–€€)

This down-to-earth place offers reasonably priced local dishes.

✉ 15 Arseniou Street ☎ 26610-33815 🕐 Lunch and dinner

Old Fortress Café (€)

At the top of the Old Fortress, with fine views of Garítsa Bay. Pastas and salads served all day. Popular spot by night.

✉ Old Fortress, Spianáda (Esplanade) ☎ 26610-48550 🕐 Daily 9am–2am

Porta Remounda (€–€€)

Very good *psarotaverna* (fish taverna). Try *soopiess* (cuttlefish).

✉ 14 Moustoxidi Street, off Kapodistriou ☎ 26610-48661 🕐 Lunch and dinner

Rex (€€–€€€)

See page 59.

To Dimarchio (€€–€€€)

Excellent mix of Greek and international cuisine and a lovely Old Town setting make this restaurant popular with locals and visitors.

✉ Plateia Dimarcheio ☎ 26610-39031 🕐 Lunch and dinner

Sagrado (€€–€€€)

A classic Old Town eatery, with a leafy courtyard where you can enjoy fine Asian-influenced dishes as well as traditional island choices.

✉ 16 Arlioti Street with Maniarizi ☎ 26610-36669 🕐 Dinner

Sze Chuan (€€)

If you like Chinese food this is the place to head for, although it's a bit out of town. All the standard dishes, but with flair.

✉ 60 Ethnikis Antistaseos ☎ 26610-26560 🕐 Dinner

Venetian Well (€€–€€€)
See page 59.

KANÓNI
Nafsika (€€)
Classy food, from lavish Greek dishes to chicken curry. Equally lavish desserts include chocolate mousse, *baklava* and *kataifi*.
✉ 11 Nafsikas, opposite Divani Hotel ☎ 26610-44354 🍽 Dinner

SHOPPING

BOOKS, NEWSPAPERS AND MAGAZINES
Kiosk
A newspaper and magazine shop behind the Liston with a large international selection from fashion magazines to hobbies.
✉ 11 Kapodistriou (behind the Liston). Also at Old Port ☎ 26610-42760

Leon Markosian
An excellent small newsagent and bookseller selling international newspapers and a good range of books, including guidebooks.
✉ 20 G Theotoki ☎ 26610-39761

Lycoudis
Wide range of books; mainly Greek publications, but with a good selection of guidebooks. Some local books translated into English, German, Italian and French. Paperback novels in English.
✉ 4 L Vrokini Street (Georgaki's Square) ☎ 26610-39845

Plou Bookshop
A Corfu institution, worth visiting for its timeless appeal. Most books are in Greek, but there are a few English-language gems.
✉ 2 Parado Nikifolou Theotoki 14 ☎ 26610-42128

CLOTHING
Backover
Quality casual wear and swimwear. Top brand names include French Connection, Calvin Klein and Henri Lloyd.
✉ 51/53 N Theotoki ☎ 26610-26735

The Beauty Shop
Cosmetics and perfumes by names such as Revlon and Estée Lauder. Also Marks & Spencer underwear.
✉ G Theotoki and Alexandras Avenue ☎ 26610-21165

The Body Shop
Branch of the international chain. English-speaking staff.
✉ St Spyrídon's Square (Plateía Iroon Kypriakou Agonos)

English Imports
Range of clothing and household goods, some non-perishable food items, English newspapers and books. Friendly staff.
✉ 1st Parados Mitropoliti Methodiou (on corner with San Rocco Square, signposted down alleyway) ☎ 26610-47692

Georgios N Kritikos
This friendly, busy shop sells every kind of scarf, hat and bag.
✉ 42 G Theotoki Street ☎ 26610-37410

Kannabishop
This shop has clothing, shoes, cosmetics, beer, skateboards and much more, all made from cannabis hemp and all perfectly legal.
✉ 46 Kalochairetou Street ☎ 26610-82175

Marks & Spencer
Stylish clothes, but don't expect bargain prices.
✉ 15–17 G Theotoki Street ☎ 26610-41360

Praxis
Always popular with the young. Levi jeans and casual wear by O'Neill and Diesel.
✉ N Theotoki

Trifouna Voula
There's a wonderful collection of linen and lacework in this small shop.
✉ 21 Filarmonikis ☎ 26610-22574

CRAFTS, ANTIQUES, JEWELLERY AND CERAMICS

Anti-Kairoi
A good selection of Greek craftwork, including embroidery, silver jewellery, as well as heavier antiques and carpets.
✉ 13 Dimarcheiou Square ☎ 26610-43090

Ex Oriente Lux
A good selection of *kombologi* (worry beads) can be found among a plethora of craft goods at this entertaining shop.
✉ 8 Kapodistriou ☎ 26610-45259

Guilford House
Very attractive showroom filled with authentic antiques.
✉ 63 Guilford Street ☎ 26610-47638

Kaltsas
This fine jeweller is popular with locals and visitors alike and offers stylish designs and top-brand watches.
✉ 28 N Theotoki Street and 41 Evgeniou Voulgareos Street ☎ 26610-23830

Kai to Ploio Fevgei
A great collection of craftwork.
✉ 109 N Theotoki Street ☎ 26610-39068

Ministry of Culture Museum Shop
Inside the entrance archway to the Old Fortress, this bookshop and gallery sells expensive art and archaeological replicas.
✉ Old Fortress ☎ 26610-46919

Mohamed Koriem Ceramics
Attractive ceramic ware and other craftwork.
✉ 56 Guilford Street (Town Hall Square) ☎ 26610-45610

Olive Wood Workshop
Carved wooden objects, both decorative and functional. Imaginative designs, large and small.
✉ 27 Filarmonikis/54 G Theotoki ☎ 26610-40621

Terracotta

This stylish shop has a good selection of jewellery, ceramics and sculptures, and specializes in contemporary Greek art and crafts.

✉ 2 Filarmonikis ☎ 26610-45260

Theofanis Sp. Lykissas

Replica icons, candles and ecclesiastical objects.

✉ 18 St Spyrídon's Square (Plateía Iroon Kypriakou Agonos) ☎ 26610-47397

FOOD AND DRINK

Andriotis

Traditional confectionery such as *mandoláto* (almond nougat), *mandoles* (burned sugared almonds), walnut chocolate, as well as bottles of Kumquat in the shape of Corfu.

✉ Arlioti Maniarizi 1 ☎ 26610-38045

Cava Paipeti

Lots of fine wines, nougat and olive-oil soap are displayed in this fine old Venetian cellar venue. Another similar shop, To Paradosiakon, is run by the same management.

✉ 7 Arlioti ☎ 26610-30778. To Paradosiakon ✉ 12 Agios Spyridonos ☎ 26610-38277

Costas Thimis

See page 77.

Kriticos

Irresistible selection of sweets to ruin any holiday diet you might forlornly be considering. Good service. Two branches.

✉ Town Hall Square ☎ (26610) 40444 ✉ G Theotoki ☎ 26610-26676

Marcos Margossian

This wonderful coffee, wine and spirit shop also sells sweets and biscuits. Courteous service.

✉ 20 G Theotoki (south side, opposite Pallas Cinema)

Nostos

Tasty cakes, pastries and desserts. Wines and spirits.
✉ St Spyrídon's Square (Plateía Iroon Kypriakou Agonos). On approach to Church of St Spyrídon ☎ 26610-47714

Starenio

Traditional bread, honey cake, and sweet biscuits of numerous delicious flavours.
✉ Guilford ☎ 26610-47370

MARKET AND MAIN SHOPPING AREAS

Fruit and Vegetable Market

Corfu Town's lively morning market beneath the walls of the New Fortress has an excellent selection of fruit, vegetables and edible olives. Fresh fish is also sold, and some clothes and souvenirs.
✉ G Markora 🕔 Mon–Sat 7–1.30

G Theotoki/Voulgareos

A range of shops of all types.
✉ Main linking streets that run northeast from San Rocco Square to the Old Town

Mitropoliti Methodiou

Middle-market clothes, shoe and hardware shops.
✉ Street running southwest from San Rocco Square

N Theotoki

Numerous fashion shops, jewellers, wines and spirits.
✉ Runs from behind the Liston towards the New Fortress

Sevastianou Street

Great selection of stylish fashion and shoe shops.
✉ Runs from behind the Liston to M Theotoki

Xenofondos Stratigou

Ships' chandlers, engineering shops and hardware shops.
✉ Main road running west between the Old Port and the New Port

ENTERTAINMENT

BARS

Cavalieri Hotel Roof Garden

The roof terrace is perfect for an evening cocktail or a light meal.

✉ 4 Kapodistriou Street ☎ 26610-39041 🕐 In season 6.30pm–1am

Magnet

A great place for relaxing over drinks or coffee to a background of mainstream, rock and Greek music.

✉ 102 Kapodistriou ☎ 26610-45295 🕐 6pm–1am

Mobile

Greek music at a friendly venue. Price of drinks is above average.

✉ 52 Eth Antistasseos Street ☎ 26610-34198 🕐 From noon onwards

Morrison Café

Located atop the New Fortress the unique style of this popular venue is enhanced with some fine jazz as well as rock and pop.

✉ New Fortress ☎ 26610-27477 🕐 6pm–early hours

Sax

The in-place for Corfu Town's younger set, with bright décor and rocking sounds. Special party nights get going after midnight.

✉ Sebastianou Street 🕐 Evening–late

CINEMAS

Greek cinemas show all the mainstream American and European films and English-language films are subtitled in Greek.

Orfeus

Smaller venue with good selection of films, usually in English with Greek subtitles.

✉ Corner of Akadimias Street and Aspioti Street ☎ 26610-39768/9

Phoenix

Open-air, summer-only cinema showing Greek and foreign films.

✉ Akadimias Street ☎ 26610-37428 🕐 Jun–Aug

CONCERTS

There are 18 marching bands, or Philharmonic Societies, on Corfu. Corfu's strong musical tradition is also maintained by the Corfu Symphony Orchestra and Choir, while the students of the Music Department of the Ionian University often perform in public.

The Esplanade

Musical performances at the bandstand, known as the Palko, on the Esplanade during the summer months. Often the venue for concerts by the Philharmonic Societies and other performers.

Old Fortress

Open-air sound and light extravaganzas during the summer. Performances are in English, Greek, French and Italian.
✉ Old Fortress, Esplanade ☎ 26610-48310/48311 ✪ Evening performance

DANCE CLUBS AND DISCOS

Corfu has many dance clubs and music bars, all of which play contemporary styles of music. The DJs in the bigger clubs are often British and they play the dance music currently popular in Northern Europe. The dance clubs and music bars of Corfu Town are concentrated on the 'Disco Strip', or 'The Straight' as it is better known, a few kilometres west of the New Port on Ethnikis Antistasseos, the main road from the town to the north and west. When travelling to and from the clubs it is probably safer to do so by taxi or bus rather than on foot. The average price for a drink is about €5. There is an admission charge at some clubs.

Aperitto

Easygoing music bar with a mix of Greek and international sounds.
✉ 40 Eth Antistasseos Street ☎ 69773-02566 ✪ Evening–late

Au Bar

A long-established, comparatively sophisticated dance club with a garden cocktail bar and good music. Go late to see it in full swing. Drinks are on the pricy side.
✉ 30 Eth Antistasseos Street ☎ 26610-34477 ✪ From midnight onwards

Ekati

Best known for its *bouzouki* band, the Ekati is a stylish, expensive and very Greek nightclub on the edge of Corfu Town. Large bar, dancing hall; dinners are available.

✉ Alíkes Potomós Street ☎ 26610-45920 🕐 Daily midnight–late; winter Fri and Sat only

Electron

Electron offers an interesting mix of Greek and European dance music in a tropical ambience. Price of drinks is above average.

✉ 28 Eth Antistasseos Street ☎ 26610-26793

Hippodrome

The club with the pool. Big venue catering for 2,000 clubbers, hopefully not all of them in the pool. There is a mix of connecting levels, both indoors and outdoors, with exotic palms and bar-top dancers. The Hippodrome is open in the mornings for coffee, drinks, food and swimming. Price of drinks is above average. The entrance fee includes one drink.

✉ 52 Eth Antistasseos Street ☎ 26610-43150 🕐 11pm onwards

Privelege

Mainstream, but cool, venue with white décor and a fairly fashionable clientele.

✉ 42 Eth Antistasseos Street ☎ 26610-80780 🕐 11pm onwards

Sodoma

For a great taste of modern Greek clubbing this is the place to squeeze into. Popular with locals and visitors alike, it showcases top Greek stars. Especially busy at weekends.

✉ 28 Eth Antistasseos Street ☎ 26610-37227 🕐 From late–dawn

THEATRE
Municipal Theatre of Corfu

Fairly regular performances by groups such as Corfu's Municipal Choir. Musical events, opera, drama and dance. Licensed bar.

✉ 68 G Theotoki ☎ 06610-37520

Northern Corfu

Northern Corfu offers the full range of the island's charms: beach resorts, hill villages, wetlands and the mighty Mount Pandokrator, whose wilder reaches provide an escape from the crowds and whose rocky eastern slopes drop steeply to quiet coves and dazzling shingle beaches.

North-coast resorts have developed rapidly to keep pace with the many holidaymakers who flock to the area and the busy coast roads are lined with bars, cafés, tavernas, shops and clubs, but it's still possible to find a flavour of an older Corfu tucked away in the back streets of many villages and resorts.

To experience the essence of Corfu you need to plan. A rental car gives independence, but responsibility. A stress-free alternative is the rural bus service. Walking can be combined with bus connections to get even closer to traditional Corfu: some of the best walking areas are on the more remote northeast coast, and the mountain trails of Mount Pandokrator.

ACHARÁVI
(AHARAVI)

A popular family resort on Corfu's north coast, Acharávi lies a short distance inland from the beach and to either side of the wide main road. The wooded heights of Mount Pandokrator rise impressively behind and a different world of dense olive groves and quiet villages, such as Epískepsi and Láfki, can be quickly, if steeply, reached from the resort.

Acharávi has a range of shops and eating places. Villas and hotels fill the space between village and seafront. The sand and shingle beach shelves gently and bathing is safe. Water sports are available here, and there are beachside cafés and tavernas. The remote Paralía Almyroú (Almirós Beach) lies at the east end of Acharávi's long strand. This is less crowded but the shoreline has low mudstone reefs, which children may find awkward and slippery.

➕ 7E ✉ 38km (23 miles) north of Corfu Town, on north coast main road 🍴 Beachside tavernas and cafés (€–€€) 🚌 Green bus from Avramiou Street, Corfu Town– Acharávi ❓ Limited parking on beachfront

ÁGIOS SPYRÍDON
(ÁGIOS SPYRÍDONAS)

Standing on a small, peaceful bay at the northeast corner of Corfu, opposite the mountainous coast of Albania, Ágios Spyrídon is reached from the main road down a lane twisting through olive groves. At one time this appealing area was relatively free of buildings, but there has been increasing development, including construction of a big hotel complex. There is a little crescent-shaped beach of fine sand. Behind lies the important wetland area of the Andinioti Lagoon, a protected wildlife site that nurtures a host of birds, insects, mammals and wild flowers. A bridge spans the lagoon outlet and leads on to Ákrotírio (Cape) Agías Aikaterínis, which is worth exploring.

Just inland from the cape, amid pine trees, is the old monastery of Agia Ekaterini (St Katherine). A track leads, in about 3km (2 miles), to Paralía Almyroú (Almirós Beach).

✚ 9F ✉ On north coast 43km (27 miles) from Corfu Town 🍴 Tavernas at Ágios Spyrídon and at Almirós (€–€€) ❓ Limited roadside parking

ÁGIOS STÉFANOS (NORTHEAST)

The fishing village of Ágios Stéfanos has kept its traditional character while adapting gracefully to its other role as a resort. Set within the arms of a quiet bay, it is reached down a road which winds through olive groves, then descends through steep bends to the coast. Early and late in the day, it feels as if the way of life that has flourished here for generations has hardly changed at all. To the east, across the narrow waters of the Corfu Channel, lies Albania, here at its closest point to Corfu. The beaches become crowded in summer when excursion boats bring day visitors from nearby Kassiópi and Kalámi. Boats and beach equipment can be rented, and some water sports are available.

Tracks and paths lead north to the isolated beach at Avláki (➤ 128). The road south ends at the very long beach of Kerasiá.

Although this is an undeveloped area – apart from a single taverna and some villas – Paralía Kerasiás (Kerasiá Beach) is very popular with day visitors, who arrive in large numbers by excursion boat.

✚ 11D ✉ 35km (22 miles) north of Corfu Town on the northeast coast. A 3km (2-mile) lane leads to the village from Siniés on the main coast road 🍴 Several tavernas (€€) 🚌 Green bus from Avramiou Street, Corfu Town–Siniés, then walk 🛥 Ágios Spyrídon and Kerasiá can both be reached from Kassiópi and other resorts by boat ❓ Limited parking

AGNI

Agni lies on the tree-shrouded northeast coast of Corfu to the south of Kalámi. A narrow lane leads for over 1km (0.5 miles) down a steep-sided valley from the main road just before Kéntroma village, but driving is not advised and it is wiser to walk down to the small beach. Agni is often reached by boat from neighbouring resorts. The tavernas here are noted for their good food, and they are popular and often busy. It is possible to walk along the coast from Agni, north to Kalámi, or south to Nissaki, passing the old chapel of St Arsenious on the way.

✚ 10C ✉ 28km (17 miles) north of Corfu Town on northeast coast 🍴 Taverna Agni (€€) 🚌 Green bus from Avramiou Street, Corfu Town–Kassiópi to main road turn-off, then 1km (0.5 miles) walk 🛥 Caiques from Kalámi and from resorts to the south ❓ Parking is very difficult

a drive around northeast Corfu

This is a route of dramatic contrasts, following Corfu's scenic northeast coast and returning through the mountains.

Start at the Old Port in Corfu Town. Drive west from Old Port along Xenofondos Stratigou and Eth Antistasseos. Continue along the coast road for 3km (2 miles) to a big junction. Go right, and after 10km (6 miles), at Tzavros, turn off right, signposted Dassiá. Pass through Dassiá (▶ 130–131), Ipsos (▶ 140) and Barmpáti (▶ 128). Pass through Nissaki (▶ 136) and 5km (3 miles) further on reach the turn off for Kalámi (▶ 44–45).

Parking is limited at Kalámi, but there is a large lay-by on the main road just before the turn off. From here it's under 1km (0.5 miles) to Kalámi and Kouloúra (➤ 135).

Continue along the main road to Kassiópi (➤ 132–133) and on to Acharávi (➤ 120). Halfway through Acharávi's wide main street, pass a walled roundabout with an old waterpump at its centre. About 150m (165yds) further on, look out for a signpost pointing left to Epískepsi and Ágios Panteleímon. Turn left on to a narrow road. Continue steeply and through many bends (watch for occasional pot-holes). In 5km (3 miles), reach Epískepsi.

Epískepsi is a traditional mountain village at the heart of olive-growing country.

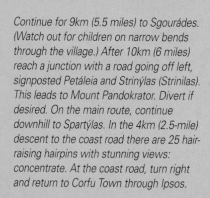

Continue for 9km (5.5 miles) to Sgourádes. (Watch out for children on narrow bends through the village.) After 10km (6 miles) reach a junction with a road going off left, signposted Petáleia and Strinýlas (Strinilas). This leads to Mount Pandokrator. Divert if desired. On the main route, continue downhill to Spartýlas. In the 4km (2.5-mile) descent to the coast road there are 25 hair-raising hairpins with stunning views: concentrate. At the coast road, turn right and return to Corfu Town through Ipsos.

Distance 80km (50 miles); 100km (62 miles) if Mount Pandokrator is included
Time 6 hours, with stops; 7–8 hours if Mount Pandokrator is included
Start/end point Corfu Town ✚ 32S
Lunch The Pump House (€–€€) ✉ Acharavi
☎ 26630-63271

ÁKROTÍRIO KOMMÉNO (CAPE KOMMÉNO)

The wooded promontory of Cape Komméno encloses a small south-facing bay at the northern end of the larger Gouviá Bay. The resort's hotels and villas are at the top end of the price range, and there is a whiff of exclusiveness in the air here.

Komméno has its own version of Kanóni's little church at Vlachérna (➤ 46–47) in the form of the church at Ypapanti on its causeway island. Several manufactured beaches lie along the wooded shores, but they are small and monopolized by hotel guests.

In 1537 and again in 1716, Turkish armies landed in the Cape Komméno and Gouviá area in ultimately unsuccessful bids to capture Venetian Corfu.

➕ 30T ✉ 11km (7 miles) north of Corfu Town. Reached from coast road north of Gouviá just after branching right from the road to Paleokastritsa 🍴 There are a number of good-quality restaurants (€€–€€€) ❓ Limited parking

ÁNO KORAKIÁNA

Áno, or Upper, Korakiána is a handsome hill village with a strong Venetian element to its buildings and its churches; it even has its own Philharmonic Society.

The village lies along the tree-covered foothills of the western massif of Mount Pandokrator (➤ 54–55). The Church of St Athanasios has an 18th-century fresco of St Spyrídon and St Athanasios banishing a dragon, the symbol of a 4th-century plague. At the village's midpoint is

the entertaining façade of a house displaying the less spiritual but highly diverting sculptures of local 'popular' artist Arestides Zach Metallinos.

The road north from here zigzags madly up the curtain wall of the mountain to Sokráki and on to the aptly named Zygós (Zigós), perched on the mountain slopes and taking its name from *zigaria*, meaning 'balance'.

✚ 7B ✉ 18km (11 miles) northwest of Corfu Town 🍽 Cafés in village (€) 🚌 Green bus from Avramiou Street, Corfu Town–Korakiána ❓ Small car park

AVLÁKI

Avláki comes as something of a surprise because of its refreshing lack of development, although it can become quite busy when day visitors arrive by excursion boat. A narrow road leads from the main road past the holiday complex of Village Michael Angelo, then winds down to the coast through olive groves and open country for just over 1km (0.5 miles). A long swathe of shingle and sand skirts the shores of a deep bay and dense olive groves cover the slopes behind. There are some villas among the trees, plus a couple of tavernas. A windsurfing and dinghy sailing centre is based here. Kassiópi and Ágios Stéfanos are reached by paths and tracks along the coast to north and south.

✚ 11D ✉ 35km (22 miles) north of Corfu Town. Turn off main coast road just before Kassiópi 🍴 Cavo Barbaro Taverna; Avláki Taverna (€–€€) 🚢 Day trips from Kassiópi (➤ 132–133) ❓ Parking behind beach and at south end

BARMPÁTI (BARBATI)

At Barbati the steep slopes of Mount Pandokrator crowd the shoreline. Behind the beach and the main road the rocky flanks of the mountain rise from dense olive groves. Barbati has a long, silvery-white, shingle beach, ideal for youngsters because it offers safe and sheltered bathing, and lies far enough below the road to escape traffic noise. Water sports include waterskiing, windsurfing and parascending, with pedaloes and dinghies for the less adventurous. The village has supermarkets, gift shops and tavernas. Nightlife is limited to quiet drinks and meals; the only thing missing on this eastern shore is a view of the sunset.

✚ 9B ✉ 20km (12.5 miles) north of Corfu Town. Beach reached down slip road at south entrance to resort 🍴 Tavernas and cafés (€–€€) 🚌 Green bus from Avramiou Street, Corfu Town–Kassiópi ❓ Limited parking on main road

DASSIÁ (DASIÁ)

Dassiá's shingle beach is spared the roadside clamour of other resorts, but its popularity and proximity to Corfu Town makes the seafront a busy place. A zone of hotels and apartments lies between the beach and the main road which has the bulk of gift shops, tavernas and services, as well as the frontages of two big hotels, the Corfu Chandris and the Dasiá Chandris. There is a popular campsite inland from the main road. The beach's shallow waters, reached down narrow lanes, make it safe for young children. Wooden jetties run seaward to cater for the boats that arrive loaded with day visitors or leave for trips. Water sports, including waterskiing and paragliding, add to the bustle, and there are beachfront café-bars and tavernas. The resort of Dafnilia at the southern end of the bay is now merged with Dassiá. About 1km

(0.5 miles) inland is Káto Korakiána, worth a visit for the Greek National Gallery Annexe of Corfu, known also as the Castello Art Gallery.
🞤 8A ✉ 13km (8 miles) north of Corfu Town on main road 🍴 Choice of cafés, snack bars on beach (€–€€) 🚌 Blue bus No 7 from San Rocco Square, Corfu Town–Dassiá 🚢 Excursions from beach 🅿 Roadside parking

GOUVIÁ

Gouviá (close to Corfu Town and therefore popular) lies on the shores of a deep bay between the horned promontories of Ákrotírio Komméno and Ákrotírio Tourka. Kondókali (► 134) lies at the southern end of the bay. Dominating part of the southern shoreline is the Gouviá yacht marina, which has increased the general activity at both resorts. The narrow shingle beach at Gouviá becomes crowded in summer, especially since ferries from Corfu Town bring in large numbers of day visitors. There is enough beach equipment and water sports, including paragliding, to suit all tastes, and bathing is very safe. The resort has numerous restaurants, tavernas, cafés, bars and shops, with the nightlife geared towards young people.

Gouviá Bay was used by the Venetians as a harbour and as a ship-repair and provisioning station.
🞤 29T ✉ 8km (5 miles) north of Corfu Town 🍴 Snack bars and tavernas (€–€€) 🚌 Blue bus 7 from San Rocco Square, Corfu Town–Kondókali–Gouviá–Dassiá 🚢 Excursion boats from Corfu Town 🅿 Parking at south end of beach near marina

KALÁMI

See pages 44–45.

KASSIÓPI

The old port of Kassiópi lies within a picturesque setting of wooded promontories. Today the village is a thriving resort but mixed in are relics of its ancient past. There was a prehistoric settlement here and a Corinthian 'city' long before the Romans colonized the site. Beneath the village church lie the remains of a temple to Jupiter Cassius, from whom Kassiópi gets its name. Wealthy Romans came here for recreation, including Cato, Cicero and Tiberius. The Romans fortified the headland above the harbour, and a castle was built in the 13th century by the Angevin rulers of Corfu. The Venetians wrecked this fortress and built one of their own, the broken walls of which still encircle the crown of the hill. Kassiópi's church is dedicated to the Blessed Virgin Kassiópitra, and possesses an icon of the Virgin that was credited at one time with having miraculous powers. This made the village a place of pilgrimage long before Spyrídon became Corfu's patron saint.

Kassiópi is a working fishing port and the harbour has a lively atmosphere. The pebble beaches are small and hidden away behind headlands.

✚ 10E ✉ 37km (23 miles) north of Corfu Town on main coast road 🍴 Large choice of snack bars and tavernas (€–€€) 🚌 Green

bus from Avramiou Street, Corfu
Town–Kassiópi  Ferry boats to and
from Corfu Town. Excursions to other
resorts **?** Very limited parking at the
harbour and at the north end of the resort
by Kalamionas Beach

KÉNTROMA (KÉNDROMA)

On the northeast coast between
the better known resorts of Nissaki
and Kalámi are a number of tiny
coves with shingle beaches; they
are reached down steep, narrow
lanes, which are unsuitable for cars,
branching off from the main road.
Kéndroma lies just to the south of
Agni (► 123) amid a coastal
landscape of tree-covered slopes
ending at rocky promontories and a
sea of exquisite blues and greens.

A short distance southwest of
Kéndroma is the Sol Elite Nisáki
Beach Hotel, beyond which is
Kamináki, another tiny cove with
nothing but a shingle beach and a
nearby taverna.

+ 10C **✕** 28km (17 miles) north of Corfu
Town on northeast coast **¶** Tavernas (€)
at coves **🚌** Green bus from Avramiou
Street, Corfu Town–Kassiópi to main road
turn-off, then 0.5km (0.3-mile) walk
🚢 Excursion boats visit **?** Parking
and turning at the beaches can be
extremely difficult

KONTÓKALI (KONDÓKALI)

Kondókali, the first resort to the north of Corfu Town, is fast becoming the service centre for the expanding marina that takes up the adjoining shoreline. The resort has an excellent range of restaurants, tavernas and bars. The narrow pebble beaches become crowded in summer. Extended and modernized, the marina has capacity for over 800 boats and is now equipped with most services and facilities, including car rental. It is the island's main base for yacht chartering. The bay on which Kondókali and its neighbour Gouviá stand was once used by the Venetians as a harbour and service port. At the northern end of the resort a lane, signposted 'Venetian Boatyard', leads to the shore and then turns left alongside the marina's perimeter fence. At the road end are the remains of a Venetian 'arsenal' or boat-repair yard, a striking collection of skeletal arches with faded Venetian motifs.

➕ 30S ✉ 7km (4 miles) north of Corfu Town 🍴 Restaurants and snack bars (€–€€) 🚌 Blue bus No 7, from San Rocco Square, Corfu Town–Kondókali–Gouviá–Dassiá ❓ Limited roadside parking

KOULOÚRA

Kouloúra is a close neighbour to Kalámi, but has a rare sense of exclusiveness, partly because there is no beach to speak of. Excursion boats visit Kouloúra, whose name derives from the Greek word for 'ring shape' or 'lifebuoy' because of the encircling shape of the tiny bay that is set against a backdrop of cypresses and pines. Its charm is enhanced by the curve of a harbour breakwater that shelters fishing boats, and by a handsome house that stands on the site of an ancient fortress and that retains the bell-tower of a medieval chapel. The house is private; its outlook is to the sea, its privacy secured by trees. On calm days, the Corfu Channel between here and Albania can seem like an inland lake. There is a very popular restaurant within the complex.

➕ 11C ✉ 31km (19 miles) north of Corfu Town 🍴 Restaurant. Also tavernas at Kalami (€€) 🚢 Excursion boats visit ❓ Very limited parking at Kouloúra; turning is awkward

NISÁKI (NISSAKI)

The coastline here, below Mount Pandokrator's steep slopes, consists of a series of tiny, rocky coves. Cafés and tavernas on the twisting main road overlook the sea, while Nissaki's main attraction, tiny, but exquisite crescents of white shingle, are reached down a surfaced lane. The luxurious Nissaki Beach Hotel, signposted from the main road, has a beach directly below it with numerous facilities that can be enjoyed by non-residents.

✚ 10B ✉ 24km (15 miles) north of Corfu Town, on the main coast road 🍴 Tavernas (€€) 🚌 Green bus from Avramiou Street, Corfu Town–Kassiópi 🛥 Excursion boats from neighbouring resorts ❓ Limited parking

PANTOKRÁTORAS (MOUNT PANDOKRATOR)

See pages 54–55.

PERÍTHEIA (OLD PERÍTHIA)

In the hidden hollows of Mount Pandokrator's upper slopes lie the ruins of old farmsteads and villages. They were established originally by Corfu's Byzantine peoples fleeing repeated pirate raids on their coastal settlements. Abandoned villages can also be found at Old Siniés and at Rou on the east side of the mountain, but Períthia is the most impressive. Today, it is being brought back to life as ruined houses are being renovated, and summer tavernas cater for visitors.

Períthia is reached by the mountain road from Néa (New) Períthia, which lies on the coast road between Kassiópi and Acharávi. About 5km (3 miles) along this mountain road from Néa Períthia, a rough track leads off left from a steep right-hand bend on the surfaced road. (This track eventually joins the road from Strinýlas to the summit of Mount Pandokrator). For Old Períthia, keep on the surfaced road to an old church at the entrance to the village, where there is limited parking.

The framework of Períthia survives within its setting of terraced fields and scattered stands of cherry, almond, oak and walnut trees. Empty houses retain their shutters and tiled roofs, but where doors and windows gape, and floorboards sag alarmingly, it is dangerous to enter.

✠ 9D ✉ 50km (31 miles) from Corfu Town on northern slopes of Mount Pandokrator. Reached from coast road at Néa Períthia 🍴 Tavernas (€€)
❓ Limited parking by road end

RÓDA

North-coast Róda is a pleasant resort with safe
bathing and a handful of tavernas and clubs. A little
harbour within a rough breakwater marks the original
fishing village, and fishing caiques still work from
here. Róda's beach, narrow and sandy, with rocky
patches, is backed by tavernas, cafés, gift shops and
clubs. Part way up the main street is the Church of
Ágios Geórgios, set in an attractive square dotted
with lemon and plane trees. On the inland side of
the main road towards Acharávi (➤ 120) are the
remains of a 5th-century Doric temple to Apollo.

✚ 7E ✉ On the north coast, 37km (23 miles) north of
Corfu Town 🍴 Cafés and tavernas (€–€€) 🚌 Green bus
from Avramiou Street, Corfu Town–Róda 🅿 Limited parking
at seafront

SIDÁRI

There are a number of good beaches at Sidári
(➤ 73). Halfway along the long main street is a little village
square, a brave fragment of old Sidári amid the glare of tourism.
There are seats, a seahorse fountain and a bandstand wreathed in
bougainvillaea and geraniums. On the north side of the square is
the cream and white Church of St Nicholas, its porch hung with
lamps and with an icon painted on its domed interior.

At the northern end of the main street a bridge crosses the
Loxida River and the road beyond runs west past villas and hotels.
Lanes between the buildings on the north side lead to beaches
which all claim to be the location of the famous Canal d'Amour.
The image of this 'Channel of Love' has worn as thin as the original
sea arch that gave rise to the name and which has long since
collapsed. Tradition claimed that if you swam through the original
arch, various romantic events would result. Today, the official Canal
d'Amour is said to be an eroded inlet at the most easterly beach on

the north-facing coast. On the other hand, some say it is the channel between a pair of sea stacks further west, where the beaches of Vithismeno, Apotripiti and Atri vie for attention.

🕂 4E ✉ 36km (22 miles) from Corfu Town on the north coast 🍴 Cafés and tavernas (€–€€) 🚌 Green bus from Avramiou Street, Corfu Town–Róda–Sidári 🚤 Excursions by boat to Kassiópi, Paleokastritsa and the Diapondía Islands, sea conditions permitting ❓ Parking behind the main street. Main street is one way

ÝPSOS (IPSOS) AND PYRGI (PIRGI)

The resorts of Ipsos and Pirgi are at the heart of Corfu's so-called 'Golden Mile', and are deservedly popular because of it. They are effectively merged by a long main strip of cafés, restaurants, tavernas, bars, discos and shops on the inland side of the busy main road that skirts Ipsos Bay. An attractive harbour marks the southern end of the resort, and the rugged slopes of Mount Pandokrator make a handsome backdrop. Favoured by the young, the resort is a lively place with a reputation for all-night clubbing. However, the facilities and the safe bathing also make it a good beach for families with young children.

➕ 8A/8B ✉ 15km (9 miles) north of Corfu Town on the coast road 🍴 Cafés and tavernas (€–€€) 🚌 Green bus from Avramiou Street, Corfu–Pirgi–Ipsos ⛴ Small boats for rent and excursion boats

HOTELS

ACHARÁVI
Acharávi Beach Hotel (€€)
Small, beachside hotel with its own swimming pool, tennis, sports
and restaurant.
✉ Overlooking beach ☎ 26630-63102/63124 ◷ May–Oct

Ionian Princess (€€)
Sizeable hotel close to beach. Gardens, swimming pool, children's
pool, playground, tennis, restaurant and in-house entertainment.
✉ Between main road and beach ☎ 26630-63135; www.ionianprincess.gr
◷ May–Oct

ÁKROTÍRIO KOMMÉNO (CAPE KOMMÉNO)
Grecotel Corfu Imperial (€€€)
See page 74–75.

ASTRAKERI
Eleni's (€€)
At the seaward end of a quiet side road, these apartments are
ideal if you have transport. The nearby Astrakeri Beach is good
for youngsters.
✉ Astrakeri ☎ 69362-9793/60141-80147 ◷ May–Oct

AVLÁKI
Bounias Apartments/Villa Alexandra (€–€€)
See page 74.

DASSIÁ (DASIÁ)
Corfu Chandris Hotel/Dassiá Chandris Hotel (€€€)
Two luxury hotels under the same management. Choice of rooms
and individual units. All modern amenities and direct access to
beach. Swimming pools, children's play area, tennis courts, all
water sports. Restaurants, bars, shops, in-house entertainment,
including open-air cinema. Courtesy bus to and from Corfu Town.
✉ Dassiá–Káto Korakíana ☎ Corfu Chandris/Dassiá Chandris
26610-97100/4; www.chandris.gr ◷ Apr–Oct

Elea Beach (€€€)

A large, modern hotel with its own beachfront and gardens. Good choice of amenities, including a nearby water-sports centre.

✉ Dassiá–Káto Korakíana ☎ 26610-93490; www.eleabeach.com
🕓 Apr–Oct

GOUVIÁ
Louis Corcyra (€€€)

Smart luxury hotel with fine gardens and beach access. Numerous amenities, including tennis, squash, volleyball, games and a swimming pool.

✉ Beachside location ☎ 26610-90196/90198; www.louishotels.com
🕓 Apr–Oct

Molfetta Beach (€€)

For a smaller, more personal place to stay, the Molfetta Beach, with its 28 rooms and garden setting, is ideal. Nothing fancy, but it's in a decent location on the shore road yet is near the centre of Gouviá.

✉ Gouviá ☎ 26610-91915; www.molfettabeach.com 🕓 Apr–Oct

Park (€–€€)

Large, modern hotel in secluded wooded area. Good amenities include a swimming pool, tennis and volleyball. Ten minutes' walk to beach.

✉ Outskirts of resort ☎ 26610-91347/91310; www.park hotel-corfu.com
🕓 Apr–Oct

KONTÓKALI (KONDÓKALI)
Kontókali Bay (€€–€€€)

Luxury-class hotel in its own gardens, with additional bungalow accommodation. Numerous amenities, including entertainment, water sports, children's club, tennis courts and swimming pools.

✉ On peninsula by beaches ☎ 26610-99000/2; www.kontokalibay.com
🕓 Apr–Oct

NISÁKI (NISSAKI)
Nissaki Beach Hotel (€€–€€€)
See page 75.

RÓDA
Róda Beach Village (€€)
Very large hotel with additional bungalow accommodation.
Swimming pools, sun terrace, tennis court. Set in large gardens
with access to the beach.
✉ Beachside near west end of resort ☎ 26630-64181/5 🕐 Apr–Sep

SIDÁRI
Alkyon Hotel (€–€€)
Rooms are simple and on the small side at this popular hotel, but
the service is excellent. Only 300m (330yds) from the lively resort
centre and 100m (110yds) from Sidári Beach. Good meals in the
restaurant; Greek dancing in the evenings.
✉ Sidári ☎ 26630-95300; www.sidarialkyon.com 🕐 Apr–Sep

ÝPSOS (IPSOS)
Ýpsos Beach (€€)
Off main road, but within a few minutes of the beach. Swimming
pool, restaurant and plenty of in-house entertainment.
✉ Outskirts of resort ☎ 26610-93232 🕐 Apr–Oct

RESTAURANTS

ACHARÁVI (AHARAVI)
Maestro (€–€€)
A lovely beachside setting for a wide-ranging traditional menu;
fish specialities, local Corfiot dishes and crêpes.
✉ Overlooking the middle of the beach ☎ 26630-63020 🕐 Lunch
and dinner

The Pump House (€–€€)
This well-run place offers tasty Corfiot specialities and has an
excellent fresh fish and seafood menu.
✉ Main Street ☎ 26630-63271 🕐 Lunch and dinner

ÁGIOS STÉFANOS (NORTHEAST)
Eucalyptus (€€)
Beside the shingle beach, this one-time olive press offers good international cuisine in a great setting. Fish is a speciality.
✉ On the north side of the bay where the approach road turns south
☎ 26630-82007 🕔 Lunch and dinner

AGNI
Taverna Agni (€€–€€€)
See page 59.

Taverna Nikolas (€€–€€€)
Picturesque setting with good Greek food.
✉ On the beach ☎ 26630-91243 🕔 Lunch and dinner

Toula's (€€–€€€)
First-class taverna at Agni. Beachside eating with fish dishes as well as meat. Try fish *mezes* to begin, followed by prawn pilaff.
✉ Overlooks beach at road end ☎ 26630-91350 🕔 Lunch and dinner

ÁNO KORAKIÁNA
Taverna Luna D'Argento (€€)
Popular all-in experience, with great traditional food accompanied by Greek dancing and – a splash of exotica – belly dancing.
✉ In village ☎ 26630-22531 (booking advised) 🕔 Dinner

AVLÁKI
Cavo Barbaro (€–€€)
See page 62.

DAFNÍLIS
Du Lac (€€–€€€)
See page 58.

DASSIÁ (DASIÁ)
Karydia (€–€€)
Traditional Corfiot food at its unpretentious best at this popular

taverna. Enjoy *pastitsada*, chargrilled dishes and other local treats.
✉ Dassiá ☎ 26610-93432 🕓 Apr–Oct Fri–Sat dinner; Nov–Mar Sun lunch

GOUVIÁ
Argo (€€)
Enjoy fish dishes and other treats on the international menu.
✉ Gouviá Marina ☎ 26610-99251 🕓 Lunch and dinner

Gorgona (€€–€€€)
See page 63.

KALÁMI
Pepes Taverna (€€)
Pepes is a traditional, family-run taverna offering good Corfiot and
fresh fish dishes. Greek dancing at weekends.
✉ At centre of village ☎ 26630-91180 🕓 Lunch and dinner

The White House (€€)
Popular for fish, sea views and literary connections: Lawrence
Durrell lived here and wrote his pastoral idyll, *Prospero's Cell*.
✉ On south side of the bay ☎ 26630-91251 🕓 Lunch and dinner

KASSIÓPI
Little Italy (€€)
The southern Italian pasta and risotto at this pleasant and popular
restaurant are at the very top of the Kassiópi menu.
✉ Kassiópi ☎ 26630-81749 🕓 Lunch and dinner

Petrino's (€€)
On the exit road from the central square, this excellent taverna
and wine bar offers traditional and international cuisine.
✉ Kassiópi ☎ 26630-81760 🕓 Lunch and dinner

KATO KORAKIÁNA
Etrusco (€€€)
See pages 58–59.

KONTÓKALI (KONDÓKALI)
Gerekos (€€€)
This top-of-the-range, yet intimate, restaurant prepares delicious dishes including Italian-influenced fish stews and chargrilled fish.
✉ Kondókali ☎ 26610-91280 ⏱ Lunch and dinner

Roula (€€–€€€)
Great fish eatery by the marina. Savour everything from anchovies to pricey but special-treat lobster, as well as other options.
✉ Kondókali ☎ 26630-91832 ⏱ Dinner

SIDÁRI
Mickey's Inn (€–€€)
A cheerful, upbeat British-style bar and eatery, Mickey's offers grills, curries, salads and much more. Friendly welcome for families.
✉ Main Street ☎ 26630-95140 ⏱ All day until late

ÝPSOS (IPSOS)
Le Grand Balcon (€–€€)
Greek food from a huge menu. Views across Ipsos Bay. Reached from Spartýlas road, or from the main coast road through a gate.
✉ On first hairpin bend of Spartýlas road above coast road junction
☎ 26610-93958 ⏱ Dinner

Viceroy Indian (€–€€)
The first Indian restaurant on Corfu. Very authentic, with wide-ranging menu and proper tandoori-oven cooking.
✉ At north end of resort, near turn off to old Venetian boatyard ☎ 26610-93814 ⏱ Dinner; closed Mon

SHOPPING

Most non-food shops in resorts close down in the winter months.

ACHARÁVI
Dala's Gold
Smart gold- and silver-jewellery shop with various designer wear.
✉ Main street, near west end of resort ☎ 26630-63684

Elea
See page 77.

KASSIÓPI
Agatha's Lace
See page 76.

RÓDA
Agricultural Co-operative of Nyfmes
Kumquat production can be seen at this workshop and there's also a shop. Mornings only; phone ahead for times of openings.
✉ Nymfes, near Róda ☎ 26630-94073

ENTERTAINMENT

DANCE VENUES AND BARS
Resorts such as Kávos, Benítses, Kassiópi and Ipsos are known for late-night dance club action. Most of the popular resorts have clubs and music bars. Bars often aim for the atmosphere of British pubs. Every dance style going, including pop, rock, house, garage, trance, drum'n bass and R&B, as well as modern Greek in clubs that are favoured by locals and Greek visitors. The Greek clubs often have the best vibe. Foam night parties are inevitable in many venues. Clubs may change hands from season to season.

ACHARÁVI
Scaravaio
Popular dance club in the main street. Looks like a wooden stockade from the outside. Inside there is a dance area, outside there is a large cocktail bar. Admission is free after midnight.
✉ Main road, by roundabout where road to Epískepsi turns off
☎ 26630-64455

DASSIÁ (DASIÁ)
Edem Cocktail Bar
Lasers and videos at this beachside venue and all-night music and dancing. Price of drinks is average. Popular daytime haunt, too.
✉ On Dassiá beach ☎ 26610-93013 🕐 10.30am–late

GOUVIÁ
Kingsize
Popular club with locals and visitors. Chill-out courtyard; covered area for dancing to latest Greek and North European sounds.
✉ Gouviá ☎ 26610-99038 ⏱ Until dawn

KASSIÓPI
Big choice of clubs and music bars including Harbour, Baron's Bar, Jasmines, Limani (see below) and Angelos.

Limani
For something a touch more relaxing, this harbourfront bar has mellow sounds to go with your cocktail, coffee or ice-cream.
✉ Kassuópi ☎ 26630-81209 ⏱ Daily

RÓDA
Domus Club
Attractive venue for daytime relaxing over coffee or drinks; also a great night-time venue with DJs playing contemporary music.
✉ Róda ☎ 26630-64474 ⏱ All day until late

SIDÁRI
Discos and dance clubs include Mint and Caesar's. The Palazzo Bar, in the centre, has a good choice of cocktails and beers from the barrel and main street Mickey's Inn is good fun.

Faros
Daytime beach bar that's transformed into one of Sidári's hottest action spots with disco classics, cabaret and karaoke. Popular with British tourists. Admission charge after 11pm, but free passes given out by day.
✉ Sidári Beach ☎ 26630-95012 ⏱ All day until late

ÝPSOS (IPSOS) AND PYRGI (PIRGI)
Still devoted to late-night fun and games, typical venues include Bar 52, Hector's, the Temple Bar, Monaco Disco, the Albatross Club, Paradise Bar and CJ's.

Northwest and Central Corfu

The northwest is an area of discovery, where roads can lead enticingly to invigorating beaches, or to the very edge of towering cliffs.

While there are plenty of family-friendly holiday resorts, it is an area that attracts those who like to get off the beaten track as well as lie on the beach. The northwest outposts of Greece, the Diapondía Islands, are clustered off this stretch of coast, and can easily be reached on a day trip by ferry.

Central Corfu boasts the beautiful west-coast resorts and the remoteness of tree-covered mountains. A rental car is a good idea for this area of Corfu, as it will allow you to explore the spectacular coasts as well as the inland villages, some seemingly untouched by time and tourism.

AFIÓNAS

The road ends at Afiónas. Go any further and you would fall into the sea. To the south of the village lies a narrow promontory that ends at Ákrotírio (Cape) Aríllas, while to the west lies Kravía (Gravia) Island, the 'Ship Island', with its little flotilla of offshore rocks. Just in front of the church at Afiónas, a surfaced lane leads off towards the cape. At a junction, the lane bears right (signed to Dionysos Taverna). Take the left branch along a track that leads out onto the promontory and down to a narrow neck of land at Porto Timoni. Here, small beaches lie to either side. On the headland are the faint remains of walls, which date from 500BC.

✚ 3B ✉ On the headland on the northwest coast 🍴 Three Brothers Taverna (€€) just before entrance to village 🚌 Green bus from Avramiou Street, Corfu Town–Magouládes–Afiónas. Not Sun ❓ Limited parking, especially mid-morning and early evening

ÁGIOS GEÓRGIOS (NORTHWEST)

Ágios Geórgios is an attractive northwest coast resort and although its individuality has been blurred by beachfront development, bold, natural surroundings still dominate the scene. The exquisite sandy beach, framed by tree-clad mountains, sweeps for over 2km (1.2 miles) along the curve of a south-facing bay between Ákrotírio (Cape) Aríllas and Ákrotírio (Cape) Falakron.

Bathing is safe here, although the area can be windy, making the resort a good windsurfing centre. There are windsurfing schools on the beach as well as jet-ski and waterski facilities.

Just inland lies Págoi (Pagi), a traditional Corfiot village, whose narrow lanes were not made for the motor car. Be warned.

✚ 3B ✉ On the shores of the bay on the northwest coast 🍴 Tavernas and restaurants (€–€€) throughout the resort 🚌 Green bus from Avramiou Street, Corfu Town–Ágios Geórgios ❓ Limited parking on beachside road

ÁGIOS STÉFANOS (NORTHWEST)

Corfu's northwest Ágios Stéfanos is a popular family resort, set on the shores of a wide bay with high, white cliffs at the northern end, and a large, flat expanse of beach. The resort, custom-built with villas, hotels, tavernas, bars and shops lining the beachfront, is named after the Chapel of San Stefano, south of the beach. Beyond the chapel is a working harbour full of fishing caiques and excursion boats. There is safe bathing at the beach, and all types of beach equipment are on offer. Water sports include waterskiing and paragliding, and trips can be arranged to the nearby Diapondía Islands (➤ 154) and south to Paleokastritsa (➤ 52–53).

✚ 2D ✉ 45km (28 miles) from Corfu Town on the northwest coast
🍴 O Manthos (€€) 🚌 Green bus from Avramiou Street, Corfu Town–Sidári–Ágios Stéfanos 🛥 Trips to Diapondía Islands and to Paleokastritsa ❓ Some parking on beach

ANGELÓKASTRO

See pages 40–41.

ARÍLLAS

This pleasant resort lies at the northern end of a long bay on the northwest coast of the island, just a few kilometres north of Ákrotírio (Cape) Aríllas. Although remote, there are plenty of resort attractions and gift shops crammed into the narrow approach road.

The narrow beach is mainly sand with patches of shingle and it has a gentle slope into the sea. The bay here can be quite breezy at times, making the resort particularly popular with windsurfers. Boards, pedaloes and canoes can be rented.

Kravía (Gravia) Island lies to the south. Like every other rocky islet off Corfu's coast, it is claimed to be the Phaeacian ship turned to stone by Poseidon in revenge for the Phaeacians transporting Odysseus home to Ithaca.

🚹 2C 📧 43km (27 miles) from Corfu Town on northwest coast. Reached from Troumbetas 🍴 Several tavernas and cafés (€–€€) 🚌 Green bus from Avramiou Street, Corfu Town–Afiónas, continues to Aríllas 🚢 Excursion boats to and from other resorts ❓ Some seafront parking

DIAPÓNTIA NISIÁ
(DIAPONDÍA ISLANDS)

Corfu's Diapondía Islands are the northwest outposts of Greece. The nearest of the three inhabited islands is Mathráki, just under 5km (3 miles) from the Corfu coast. The two others are Eríkoussa and Othoní.

The Diapondías have a long history; flint tools of the early Stone Age, the neolithic and the Bronze Age have been discovered on all of them, and for centuries they were important refuges for ships. At times they were also probably home to pirates. Othoní, the largest of the group, is claimed by some to be Calypso's island from which Odysseus eventually escaped, only to be shipwrecked at Érmones (➤ 156–157), on the coast of ancient Corfu.

All the islands have beaches and there are some tourist services, including a few tavernas and rooms to let – but choice is very limited. Mathráki is the handsomest of the islands, deeply wooded and with a very long beach. Othoní has several beaches including Aspri Ammos, meaning the 'white sand', on its western shore. Eríkoussa, the busiest of the three, has a long curving beach in front of its main settlement, Porto.

✚ 1E (off map) ✉ 5–15km (3–9 miles) northwest of Corfu 🍴 Mathráki: café (€); Othoní: tavernas (€), restaurant (€€); Eríkoussa: beachside taverna (€)
🚢 Excursions from Sidári and from Ágios Stéfanos (northwest) daily during season, depending on sea conditions. There are regular ferries from Corfu Town and from Ágios Stéfanos. Contact San Stefano Travel ☎ 26630-51910. The crossing can sometimes be quite lively in these open waters

DOUKÁDES

This archetypical Corfiot mountain village lies beneath dramatic limestone crags, with a steep hinterland of lovely olive groves. Viewed from the Troumbetas Pass road, the great cliff above the clustered village seems to hang in mid-air. Doukádes has a pretty central square with adjacent tavernas and shops and there are seats alongside the Church of the Blessed Virgin Mesochoritissa, notable for its splendid doorcases and doors. Numerous Venetian buildings of great style grace the village.

✚ 5A ✉ 18km (11 miles) northwest of Corfu. From the Paleokastritsa road, go through village to a small car park reached down a slip road to the left 🍴 Elizabeth's Taverna (€) 🚌 Green bus from Avramiou Street, Corfu Town–Paleokastritsa, then short steep walk ❓ In late June there is a festival at Doukádes in celebration of St John

ÉRMONES

Picturesque Érmones Bay has a strong claim to being the place where Homer's Odysseus was washed ashore after his voyage from Calypso's isle. Here Odysseus was discovered by the beautiful Nausicaa, daughter of Alcinous, King of the Phaeacians – the legendary inhabitants of Scheria, ancient Corfu.

Érmones lies between two steep headlands, with its shingle beach lapped by dazzling turquoise water. The Rópa River runs into the bay across the middle of the beach and this feature has strengthened the Homeric associations still further. Here Nausicaa and her hand-maidens came to wash clothes 'in the flowing stream of the lovely river', and, while playing a form of classical beach ball, discovered the exhausted Odysseus lying on the beach.

There has been much development of hotels and apartments at Érmones in recent years, and today, beach ball is just one of numerous activities on offer. These include paragliding, and there are several tavernas above the beach.

The beach shelves quickly into deep water and this should always be kept in mind when young children and poor swimmers are swimming in the sea at Érmones.

A rough path leads in a northerly direction from the place where the road ends above the beach, along the northern arm of the bay to the little Church of Zoodochos Pighi (Source of Life). Here there are fine views to a lonely headland.

Situated inland from Érmones, on the green flatlands of the Rópa Valley, is the Corfu Golf and Country Club, where a meandering stream adds a touch of zest to the golf course.

🚌 27R ✉ 17km (10.5 miles) from Corfu Town on west coast. Reached from Rópa Valley, through Vátos 🍽 Nausika Restaurant Bar (€–€€) 🚌 Green bus from Avramiou Street, Corfu Town–Vátos 🚢 Excursion boats to and from other resorts ❓ Limited parking above beach

GLYFÁDA (GLIFADA)

Glyfáda, one of the finest beaches on the west coast of Corfu, with a long stretch of golden sand, is reached down a winding road. There has been much development here and major hotels tend to dominate the backdrop of tree-covered coastal hills. Water sports of every kind are available, and these include sailing and windsurfing. The beach shelves steeply in places, but otherwise Glyfáda is the kind of sandy paradise adored by youngsters. Tavernas line the beachfront and popular venues such as the Aloha Beach Club go non-stop until late into the night. You can find some peace and quiet along tracks and paths to the north and south of the resort.

➕ 28Q ✉ 16km (10 miles) from Corfu Town 🍴 Beachside tavernas (€–€€)
🚌 Green Bus from Avramiou Street, Corfu Town–Vátos–Glyfáda
🚢 Excursion boats from neighbouring resorts ❓ Car park behind beach

MAKRÁDES

The little village of Makrádes lies on the road north from Paleokastritsa at the junction with the lane to Kríni and the fortress of Angelókastro (➤ 40–41). Makrádes works very hard at being the retail hub of the known world. Roadside stands and their insistent traders, selling everything from embroidered table linen to knitwear, ceramics and carpets, lie in wait for summer coach parties, while tavernas and cafés help you to get rid of the small change.

Just before Makrádes is Lákones, the village with the view to beat all views. It stands high above Paleokastritsa at the end of a wild series of rising S-bends, with breathtaking views of the west coast.

➕ 3A ✉ 35km (22 miles) northwest of Corfu Town 🍴 Cafés and tavernas (€€) 🚌 Green bus from Avramiou Street, Corfu Town–Makrádes
❓ Roadside parking

MYRTIÓTISSA (MIRTIOTISSA)

Beautiful Myrtiótissa, with its backdrop of tree-covered cliffs, was once a genuine 'desert island' beach, praised by novelist Lawrence Durrell for its 'lion-gold' sand. The south end is favoured by nudists. Difficult access and the cliffs behind the beach have discouraged permanent development – the only blot being the line of telegraph poles and wires that lead to the **Monastery of the Blessed Virgin Myrtiótissa.** It was founded in response to the discovery, in a myrtle bush, of an abandoned icon of the Virgin. The monastery has fine arched doorways and carved keystones, which contrast with the food cans used as flowerpots in the forecourt. The beach shelves slightly and there are offshore reefs and rocks of very rough conglomerate. Beware of currents running offshore.

➕ 28R ✉ 12km (7.5 miles) west of Corfu Town. Reached down a 1km (0.5-mile) track, signposted from the Glyfáda road, or by a 2.5km (1.5-mile) path from the village of Vátos 🍴 Snack bar on beach (€) summer only and Myrtiótissa restaurant (€) uphill from the beach 🚌 Green bus from Avramiou Street, Corfu Town–Vátos 🚤 Excursion boats arrive from other resorts ❓ Parking at beach is very limited

Monastery of the Blessed Virgin Myrtiótissa
🕐 Daily 8–1, 5–8

PALAIOKASTRÍTSA (PALEOKASTRITSA)

See pages 52–53.

PÉLEKAS

This hilltop village has evolved into something of an inland tourist resort due to the popularity of nearby Glyfáda on the coast and of small beaches, such as Kontoyialos and Gialiskari. Above the village is a famous viewpoint, known variously as the Kaiser's Lookout, Tower or Throne, up a steep road signposted from the centre of Pélekas. It was a favourite spot of the German emperor Kaiser Wilhelm II in the early 20th century. The views are spectacular; east to Corfu Town; northwest along the Rópa Valley; south to Mount Ágios Matthéos; and west to the western sea.

Pélekas itself retains the charm of a typical Corfiot hill village, although development has begun to erode its traditional character. There are several tavernas and cafés, plus numerous shops and tourist agencies. In the central square, with its war memorial and well-kept church, an old sea mine serves as an eccentric plant pot.
➕ 29Q ✉ 13km (8 miles) from Corfu Town on west coast 🍴 Jimmy's (€€)
🚌 Blue bus No 11 from San Rocco Square, Corfu Town–Pélekas ❓ Limited parking in village. Parking at viewpoint

PEROULÁDES

Corfu's northwestern limits are marked by the dramatic white cliffs of Ákrotírio (Cape) Drástis, near the village of Perouládes, which rise sheer from the sea to heights of over 50m (165ft) in places. Long, narrow fins of rock jut out from the shore and gentler promontories, patched with scrub, mark the far points of land. From the village square, complete with old water pump, a narrow road runs west between huddled buildings. A few metres along the road a lane runs steeply uphill to the right, leading past the village school and church and on to Ákrotírio Drástis. Although the lane is surfaced at first, it soon becomes very rough, and driving along it is not advised. The track leads in about 1.5km (1 mile) to a dramatic viewpoint overlooking the Diapondía Islands (► 154) to the northwest. The narrow road at Perouládes leads through the village to a right turning, signposted Longas Beach. This leads shortly to the Panorama Taverna, from where concrete steps descend to a narrow beach below towering cliffs.

✚ 3E ✉ 45km (28 miles) from Corfu Town on northwest coast 🍽 Panorama Taverna (€€) 🚌 Green bus from Avramiou Street, Corfu Town–Sidári–Perouládes–Ágios Stéfanos ❓ Limited parking in village. Parking above Longas Beach

HOTELS

ÉRMONES
Sunmarotel Érmones Beach (€€€)
Bungalow-style accommodation on terraced hillside with stairway
or funicular ride to beach. Indoor and outdoor pools, gym, tennis
and water sports. In-house entertainment, restaurant, bars.
✉ Overlooks beach ☎ 26610-94241/94243; www.sunmarotelermones.gr
🕐 Apr–Oct

GLYFÁDA
Glyfáda Beach (€€)
Small, family-run hotel with basic but good facilities and not far
from the beach.
✉ North end of resort ☎ 26610-94257/8 🕐 Apr–Oct

Louis Grand Hotel (€€€€)
Very large and luxurious hotel at far end of beach. Gardens and
beach access. Many amenities, including tennis and a range of
water sports. Restaurants, bars, shops.
✉ South end of beach ☎ 26610-94140/5; www.louishotels.com 🕐 Apr–Oct

LÁKONES
Golden Fox (€€)
See page 74.

PALAIOKASTRÍTSA (PALEOKASTRITSA)
Akrotiri Beach (€€–€€€)
See page 74.

Hotel Apollon (€€)
A well-kept resort hotel, nicely refurbished and located just across
the road from Ágios Spyrídon beach at Paleokastritsa. Friendly
service, pleasant rooms and an upbeat style make this a good
choice at the busy heart of the resort.
✉ Paleokastritsa ☎ 26630-41211; www.corfu-apollon-hotel.com
🕐 Apr–Oct

PÉLEKAS

Levant (€€)

Its hilltop location near the Kaiser's Lookout (➤ 160) means there are fabulous views of the sea from this small hotel. Rooms are pleasantly decorated and the hotel has an in-house restaurant.

✉ Above Pélekas ☎ 26610-94230; www.levanthotel.com ⏰ Apr–Nov

Villa Myrto (€–€€)

Near the lovely Myrtiótissa Beach, these well-appointed rooms with a kitchen are well run and there's a friendly welcome.

✉ Pélekas ☎ 26610-95082 ⏰ Mar–Oct

PEROULÁDES

Villa de Loulia (€€€)

See page 75.

RESTAURANTS

ÁGIOS STÉFANOS (NORTHWEST)

Symposium (€€–€€€)

This interesting eatery makes an imaginative bid to re-create the ancient eating habits and tastes of classical Greece. Good use of herbs and less common ingredients such as pinenuts and lentils.

✉ Inland from beach ☎ 69377-35595 ⏰ Apr–Oct

Taverna O Manthos (€–€€)

Dine out overlooking the beach from the garden restaurant. Corfiot specialities and barbecue food.

✉ At the north end of the seafront ☎ 26630-52197 ⏰ Lunch and dinner

DOUKÁDES

Elisabeth's (€)

See page 62.

ÉRMONES

Nausika Restaurant Bar (€–€€)

Great sunsets, great traditional food and live music.

✉ River southside, overlooking beach ☎ 26610-94236 ⏰ Lunch and dinner

GLYFÁDA (GLIFADA)
Aloha Beach Club (€)
Music bar; inexpensive restaurant with breakfast, lunch and *mezes* in the evening.
✉ Immediately south of entrance to beach ☎ 26610-94380 🕐 10am until late evening

LÁKONES
Golden Fox (€€)
Stunning setting overlooking Paleokastritsa with views to the coast. International menu, also a snack bar and swimming pool.
✉ On the road to Makrádes ☎ 26630-49101/2 🕐 Lunch and dinner

PALAIOKASTRÍTSA (PALEOKASTRITSA)
The Rock (€–€€)
The terrace of this popular restaurant, Bráxos (The Rock) is on a rocky outcrop overlooking the sea. Tasty, traditional Corfiot dishes.
✉ Harbour, Paleokastritsa ☎ 26630-41128/41233 🕐 Lunch and dinner

PÉLEKAS
Jimmy's (€€)
Jimmy and his family have been serving traditional Corfiot food here for over 25 years. Nicely furnished rooms with fine views.
✉ Pélekas village ☎ 26610-94284 🕐 Lunch and dinner

Sunset Restaurant (€€–€€€)
High living at a top level. Eat on the terrace of this stylish hotel while the sun sets. Mediterranean cuisine to suit all tastes.
✉ By Kaiser's Lookout ☎ 26610-94230 🕐 Lunch and dinner

SHOPPING

AFIÓNAS
Kir Art
Fascinating gallery and workshop as you approach Ágios Geórgios from Afiónas. Original artwork in stainless steel and olive wood.
✉ Afiónas ☎ 26630-51925

LÁKONES
The Golden Fox
The Golden Fox also has a shop selling local crafts.
✉ Lákones ☎ 26630-49108

LIPÁDES
Agrotiki Kerkyras
Local wine, herbs and honey on sale at this old mill building.
✉ Lipádes

MAKRÁDES
Makrádes (► 158) is well known for its roadside traders.
✉ Main road, 35km (22 miles) northwest of Corfu Town

ENTERTAINMENT

ARÍLLAS
Coconut Bar
There's a terrific selection of cocktails to choose from at this popular bar where English DJs play a mix of new and old hits.
✉ Main Street ☎ 26630-51150 ⏰ Until the early hours

GLYFÁDA (GLIFADA)
Aloha Beach Club
All-day venue with dance music. Restaurant offering breakfast, lunch and *mezes* in the evening. Wine from barrel. Drinks pricey.
✉ By entrance to beach ☎ 26610-94380 ⏰ 10am until late

PALAIOKASTRÍTSA (PALEOKASTRITSA)
La Grotta
Great café-bar in a rocky cove and with a veranda overlooking the sea. Down steps opposite the Hotel Paleokastritsa. Swimming.
✉ Paleokastritsa ☎ 26630-41006 ⏰ All day

PÉLEKAS
Banana Club
Open-air dancing all night, old and new dance music. Free entry.
✉ On the road to Glyfáda

Southern Corfu

The low-lying southern part of Corfu is less developed for tourism than the north and it has long stretches of peaceful beaches, though there are a few big resorts, including the lively, party resort of Kávos. Inland, this is more of a farming area, populated with fascinating villages where the life of Old Corfu goes on unhindered.

Rental bikes can be used for the many off-road tracks on Corfu. Some of the least hilly areas are in the south, around Lake Korissión and Lefkímmi, but, anywhere on the island, you should be prepared for rough surfaces, pot-holes and steep climbs. The southern tip of Corfu, Akrotíro (Cape) Asprókavos, is the recommended starting point for the Corfu Trail, a 200km (124-mile), fully marked walk crossing the whole island, detailed in *The Companion Guide to the Corfu Trail* by Hilary Whitton Paipeti or on the website (**www**.corfutrail.com).

ACHILLEÍO (ACHILLEION PALACE)
See pages 36–37.

ÁGIOS GEÓRGIOS (SOUTHWEST)
Like its northern namesake, this Ágios Geórgios has been tacked on to a long stretch of sandy beach, part of the almost continuous 12km (7.5-mile) strand that fringes the southwest coast of Corfu. Linear development has left the resort without much heart, but location is what matters. Numerous water sports are available and there are several good tavernas overlooking the beach. The beach is narrow, but you can find uncrowded space if you are willing to walk along the open coast in either direction.

On the main road, inland, is the village of Argyrádes (Argirádes), worth visiting for its Venetian architecture, its shops and cafés.

🕂 18J ⊠ On the southwest coast 🍴 Several good restaurants and tavernas (€–€€) or Kafesas (€€€) for seafood at the south end of the resort 🚌 Green bus from Avramiou Street, Corfu Town– Argirádes–Ágios Geórgios ❓ Limited roadside parking

ÁGIOS GÓRDIS
This is an attractive west-coast resort at the foot of spectacular pine-covered coastal hills. The beach is framed by big headlands to north and south; at the northern end are Plitíri Point and the rocky heights of Aerostato, known at one time as 'The Lookout' because of its use as a watch-point for pirates and potential invaders. Just offshore from Ágios Górdis's southern headland is a remarkable tusk-like pinnacle called the Ortholith.

Onshore is a similar pinnacle, beyond which rises Mount Garoúna. The beach is wide and sandy with patches of shingle, and numerous water sports are available, including a beachside diving centre. A steep hike to the south from Ágios Górdis takes you to the rocky cove of Fieroula and on to the hamlet of Pentátion.

🚌 30P ✉ 17km (10.5 miles) southwest of Corfu Town 🍴 Cafés and tavernas (€–€€) throughout resort 🚍 Green bus from Avramiou Street, Corfu Town–Ágios Górdis ❓ Limited parking at beach, but car park before road end

ÁGIOS MATTAÍOS (ÁGIOS MATTHÉOS)

There is an enduring belief that in Ágios Matthéos local people are descended from the Byzantine defenders of nearby Gardíki Castle (➤ 174–175).

The village, one of the largest and most traditional of Corfu's mountain villages, is built on a series of terraces on the tree-covered slopes of the 463m (1,519ft) Mount Ágios Matthéos, known locally as Grava. Near the top of the mountain is the 4th-century Monastery of Pandokrator, now abandoned but still cared for by the villagers. On 6 August each year a religious festival is held here through the night.

A paved lane winds through the heart of the village to a wide square with a fountain and a well-kept church. The view east across the island from here is exhilarating.

✚ 16M ✉ 22km (13.5 miles) southwest of Corfu Town 🍴 Snack bars (€) in main street 🚌 Green bus from Avramiou Street, Corfu Town–Ágios Matthéos ❓ A small car park on the northern edge of the village, signposted

ÁKROTÍRIO ASPRÓKAVOS (CAPE ASPRÓKAVOS)

Beyond the liveliness of Kávos, with its numerous bars and clubs (➤ 176–177), there is an altogether different world. At the south end of the resort a road branches left to Pantatika, the final beachside extension of Kávos. Beyond, a rough track branches right into olive groves and within seconds you are in a world of shaded trees and peace and quiet – provided it is not the height of the shooting season.

Keep to the main track as it winds on through deep woods of olive, cypress, ilex and oak, towards Cape Asprókavos. It reaches the coast above pale sandstone cliffs and finally leads to the ruin of the ancient Moní Panagiás (Monastery of Panagia Arkoudilla). Here, the Venetian bell-tower survives, framed between tall cypresses. Inside the building there are faded wall-paintings and a handful of icons.

✚ 23G ✉ 50km (31 miles) south of Corfu Town, 2km (1.2 miles) from southern end of Kávos 🍴 Wide choice of snack-bars, cafés in Kávos (€) 🚌 Green bus from Avramiou Street, Corfu Town–Kávos

ALYKÉS (ALIKES)

The Alykés salt pans, reached by road from Áno (Higher) Lefkímmi, lie on the eastern shore of the Bay of Lefkímmi. They were once exploited by the Venetians and now large numbers of migrating birds are attracted to the disused pools in spring and autumn.

➕ 21K ✉ 32km (20 miles) south of Corfu Town via Áno Lefkímmi
🍽 Beachfront taverna (€) at Petrakis ❓ Parking at road end by salt pans

BENÍTSES

There are two Benítses: brash resort and traditional Greek village. Old Benítses is an absolute delight. *Caiques* (light fishing boats), laden with nets, lie with their bows towards the harbour quays. The village square is a mix of Venetian buildings and two-storeyed houses and tavernas. A short distance north from the square, a narrow alleyway (signposted 'Roman Baths') leads to a lemon grove and the fascinating ruins of the bathhouse of a Roman villa. The old village extends inland and amid the citrus trees is a fine old church. The Corfu Shell Museum at the northern entrance to Benítses is worth a visit. It is one of the biggest and best-curated collections of shells from world-wide locations.

Resort Benítses lies south of the old village, beyond the tiny roadside Church of St Dimitrious with its single bell-tower and tiled roof. The resort is a busy social hub during the summer. The resort's reputation has mellowed, although the clubs and bars are still lively. The beach is a narrow shingle strip with the busy main road alongside. All types of water sports are available; a sizeable marina is under construction at Benítses and it should reinvigorate the village.

➕ 31P ✉ 13km (8 miles) south of Corfu Town on the main road 🍽 Paxinos Taverna (€€), just inside the Old Village 🚌 Blue bus 6, from San Rocco Square, Corfu Town–Pérama–Benítses 🚢 Excursion boats ❓ Toilets at village square. Car parking at north and south ends of resort

Corfu Shell Musem

✉ Benítses ☎ 26610-72227 🕐 Daily 10–8 💰 Moderate 🍽 Café (€)

BOÚKARIS

South of Moraïtika and Mesongí the main road
swings inland and then runs down the centre
of the island. An alternative road south from
Messongí hugs the east coast and leads past
numerous tiny roadside beaches and rocky
coves before turning inland at Boúkaris.

There is a small beach at Boúkaris, which
has a jetty, and a beachside taverna with
thatched umbrella awnings. A rough track
continues south along the coast and can be
walked or cycled for about 2km (1.2 miles) to
the fishing village of Petrití, where some
impressively large trawlers moor alongside
small caiques in a busy working harbour.

🔢 19K ✉ 23km (14 miles) south of Corfu Town on
minor coast road from Messongí 🍴 Boúkaris Beach
Taverna (€–€€) ❓ Roadside parking

GARDÍKI

The Gardíki region lies between Mount Ágios
Matthéos (► 170) and Lake Korissión
(► 48–49) and is home to some remarkable
historic remains. The most substantial is
Gardíki Castle, a ruined Byzantine fortress,
which probably dates from the early 13th
century. Near Gardíki Castle on the road from
Paramonas and Cape Varka is the Grava
Gardíkiou rock shelter, dating from the Upper
Palaeolithic period of 20,000BC, a time when
Corfu was part of what is now mainland
Epirus. During this period, primitive hunter-
gatherers used such rock shelters while on
hunting trips. Many stone tools and animal

bones have been found at Grava Gardíkiou and the site is now accessible to the public. A prominent roadside notice board indicates the site, which is about 400m (1,300ft) uphill through olive groves. Orange arrows, on brown metal signs pinned to the trees, point the way. The cave may seem mundane, but its antiquity creates a powerful sense of the past. Just up the road, a more modest sign indicates an old fountain built by Serbian soldiers in 1916.

Lake Korissión is reached by continuing from the fortress to the scattered hamlet of Gardíki, from where a side road leads to the north end of the lake. A short distance further on from the Lake Korissión turn, a track leads down to the isolated Kanouli and Alonáki beaches. Alonáki has several small fishing boats, which are launched down ramps.

🚹 16L ✉ 25km (15 miles) south of Corfu Town. Reached from the main road 1km (0.5 miles) beyond Messongí 🍴 Alonáki Beach Taverna (€) 🚌 Green bus from Avramiou Street. Corfu Town–Ágios Matthéos. Get off at Gardíki turn, then short walk ❓ Limited roadside parking by castle

KÁVOS

Kávos is Corfu's premier resort for loud and often exhibitionist holidaymaking, although no one is too lively at midday thanks to the previous night's sessions in the dozens of bars and clubs. Kávos is definitely for young, uninhibited adults, with a majority of British among them, and the first thing anyone looking for local colour will notice is the total lack of the Greek language on signs. The resort has effectively overwhelmed itself and its everyday facilities with full-on frantic boozing and partying. The sun rises on some unlovely sights after each night's excess. Not for the fastidious, but definitely for the 'funster', although you need to be fairly sharp yourself to handle a few hard-edged operators. There is a 2km-long (1.2-mile) beach, the plusses being safe bathing and plenty of water sports and other diversions.

An older Kávos survives in the forms of a handful of small fishing boats that keep their distance on offshore moorings. The beach peters out to the south, where low cliffs begin. Beyond are the lonelier reaches of Ákrotírio (Cape) Asprókavos, if you feel in need of some solitude.

✚ 23H ✉ 45km (28 miles) south of Corfu Town at end of main road south
🍴 Snack-bars and tavernas (€–€€) 🚌 Green bus from Avramiou Street,
Corfu Town–Kávos 🚢 Excursion/rental boats ❓ Limited roadside parking

LEFKÍMMI

The far south of Corfu may have Kávos as a major resort, but the true character of the area is epitomized by the town of Lefkímmi – a straggle of communities, including Melikia, Potami, Anaplades and Ringlades, that have merged into one. Lefkímmi, or 'Ta Lefki' to locals, is the commercial centre of the south's farming and vine-growing area, and reflects the everyday life beyond the beaches. Today, Lefkímmi is bypassed by a two-lane highway which hurtles south to Lefkímmi Port where it ends at the entrance to a vast quayside. From here ferries leave for Igoumenítsa on the mainland and for Paxos (➤ 100–101).

Áno (Higher) Lefkímmi is the first part of the town entered from the north. By the roadside is the handsome Church of St Arsenios. Arsenios (AD876–953) was the first Archbishop of Corfu. The south end of the long main street is dominated by the tall bell-tower of the Church of St Theodoros. Beyond is Potami, with the attractive 'Kampouli' Square and the River Himaros. The riverside roads lead to the river-mouth, where there are small beaches and sand dunes.

✚ 21J ✉ 40km (25 miles) south of Corfu Town 🍴 Maria's Taverna, Potami (€) 🚌 Green bus from Avramiou Street, Corfu Town–Kávos ❓ Roadside parking. Lefkímmi Festival, 8 July

LÍMNI KORISSIÓN (LAKE KORISSIÓN)

See pages 48–49.

MESSONGÍ (MESONGÍ)

Separated from Moraïtika by the Messongí River, Messongí is the first resort south of Corfu Town to escape from the main road. The coast sweeps away in a gentle curve to the south where tree-covered hills fill the horizon. The narrow sand and shingle beach has safe bathing and is ideal for families; a narrow road, with shops and tavernas, leads from the north end to the river bank.

South from Messongí, a coastal road leads to Boúkaris (➤ 174) past a number of good fish tavernas. Apart from relaxed meals in the evenings, there is very little nightlife. For restless youth, there are the livelier attractions of nearby Moraïtika, while the clubs of Benítses are only 8km (5 miles) to the north.

🚹 17L ✉ 22km (13.5 miles) south of Corfu Town 🍴 Cafés and tavernas (€–€€) 🚌 Green bus from Avramiou Street, Corfu Town–Kávos or Corfu Town–Messongí 🚢 Excursion boats to other resorts ❓ Roadside parking

MORAÏTIKA

The name Moraïtika sounds convincingly Hawaiian and the resort does its best to live up to the image: the beach has lots of exotic palms and thatched umbrellas. The only thing missing is the surf.

Áno (Upper) Moraïtika, a delightful complex of old houses, modern villas, and a couple of tavernas, all swamped in bougainvillaea, is tucked away on the high ground above the north end of the resort. The dusty main road of the resort proper is lined with restaurants, tavernas, bars, clubs, cafés and shops.

Between road and sea is a broad swathe of land, dotted with villas and hotels, that runs down to Moraïtika's long stretch of sun-trapping sand and shingle beach. The southern end of the beach is dominated by the very large Messongí Beach Hotel, which has its own gymnasium, tennis court, swimming pools, restaurants, beach taverna, café and shopping centre. There are water sports in plenty at Moraïtika, including gentler alternatives for children. The beach even has freshwater shower points and a changing stall at its midpoint.

✚ 17L ✉ 20km (12 miles) south of Corfu Town, on main coast road
🍽 Cafés and tavernas on beach and in main street (€–€€) 🚌 Green bus from Avramiou Street, Corfu Town–Kávos and Corfu Town–Messongí
⛴ Excursion boats from beach 🅿 Parking in main street

PÉRAMA

Lying on a steep, wooded shoreline beyond the busy suburb of
Vrioni, but not out of earshot of the airport across the adjoining
Chalkiopoúlou Lagoon, Pérama is the first resort to the south of
Corfu Town. Shingle beaches are reached down steep steps from
the main road and, in spite of their small size, offer all sorts of

facilities and most water sports. Pérama has numerous hotels, bars and gift shops and is well placed for regular bus connections, south to Benítses and beyond, and north to Corfu Town. The Achilleion (➤ 36–37) and the charming but busy Gastoúri village are only 3km (2 miles) inland to the south.

About 2km (1.2 miles) south on the coast road are the remains of the 'Kaiser's Bridge', an elaborate pierhead built by Kaiser Wilhelm II to facilitate landing from the imperial yacht.

🚏 31Q ✉ 7km (4 miles) south of Corfu Town. On main coast road to Benítses 🍴 Cafés and restaurants (€–€€) 🚌 Blue bus No 6 from San Rocco Square, Corfu Town–Pérama–Benítses ❓ Parking is difficult

PERIVÓLI

This is another of Corfu's down-to-earth farming villages, with its narrow lanes and alleyways, on the main road south. The church is called Agii Saranda (Forty Saints), a name shared with the Albanian port of Agii Saranda, dedicated in honour of 40 Christian soldiers who were martyred for their faith in the 4th century.

Perivóli has a number of traditional *kafenions* and tavernas which only *aficionados* of Greek living will feel at ease in. The village is the gateway to several accessible points on the great sweep of beach that runs down the southwest coast. These include Paralía Gardénos (Vitaládes Beach) reached through Vitaládes, and Paralía Agías Varváras (Santa Barbara Beach), also with beachside tavernas.

🚏 20J ✉ 35km (22 miles) south of Corfu Town, on main road south to Lefkímmi and Kávos 🍴 Tavernas at Vitaládes Beach and at Santa Barbara Beach (€) 🚌 Green bus from Avramiou Street, Corfu Town–Kávos ❓ Limited roadside parking. Some parking at beaches

SINARÁDES

This is another traditional Corfiot village, part Venetian, part Byzantine, with an authentic flavour of everyday island life. In the main street there is a medieval bell-tower of unpainted stone, its twin bells still in place. The village square is attractive, with huge palm trees, a small bandstand and a fountain adorned with statues of rearing horses. Sinarádes has its own Philharmonic Orchestra and the square is the focus of some excellent local festivals.

A short distance along the main street south from the square is the Church of St Nicholas. Opposite, a signpost points the way up a paved alley to the delightful **Folklore Museum of Central Corfu,** a two-storeyed building reached by a narrow stairway. Part of the building is a reconstruction of a 19th-century village house, complete with furnishings and utensils. The exhibits include musical instruments, farming tools and traditional costumes.

✠ 30P ✉ 15km (9 miles) from Corfu Town on the west coast

🍴 Cafés and tavernas (€–€€)

🚌 Green bus from Avramiou Street, Corfu Town–Sinarádes–Ágios Górdis

Folklore Museum of Central Corfu

☎ 26610-54962 🕐 All year Tue–Sun 9.30–2.30. Opening hours are flexible 🚫 Inexpensive

HOTELS

ÁGIOS GEÓRGIOS (SOUTHWEST)
Golden Sands Hotel (€)
At the centre of the long, straggling resort looking towards the sea. Handsome little church opposite in big open area adds a sense of spaciousness. The hotel has a swimming pool, children's play area, restaurant and bar.

✉ Centre of resort ☎ 26620-51225 ⏰ Apr–Oct

Villa Margaritta (€€)
These attractive two-room apartments are well-appointed and brightly decorated. There are pleasant gardens and the beach is just across the road.

✉ Ágios Geórgios ☎ 26620-51190 ⏰ Apr–Oct

ÁGIOS GÓRDIS
Ayios Gordios Hotel (€–€€)
Hotel set below spectacular coastal mountains in its own gardens and with beach access. There is a swimming pool, tennis court and games.

✉ Overlooking beach ☎ 26610-53320/53322 ⏰ Apr–Oct

ALYKÉS (ALIKES)
Iberostar Kerkyra Golf (€€€)
Large, revamped, modern hotel offering numerous facilities including swimming pools, water sports, tennis, beach area, restaurants, bars and nightclub.

✉ On main road 3km (2 miles) north of Corfu Town centre ☎ 26610-24030; www.louishotels.com ⏰ May–Oct

BENÍTSES
Iberostar Regency Beach Hotel (€€€)
Big hotel south of Benítses with extensive sports facilities and access to beach below road. There is a beachside taverna as well as a restaurant.

✉ South of Benítses ☎ 26610-71211/7; www.louishotels.com
⏰ Apr–Oct

San Stefano (€€–€€€)

Modern hotel with rooms, apartments and bungalows, in a good position above resort. Large swimming pool, tennis, playground, restaurants, bars and shops. Courtesy bus to and from beach.

✉ Above Benítses ☎ 26610-71112/8 🕐 Apr–Oct

KÁVOS
San Marina (€€)

Alongside narrow beach but some distance from centre of resort. Swimming pool and water sports and other activities organized.

✉ South end of resort ☎ 26620-61346 🕐 May–Oct

MESONGÍ (MESSONGÍ)
Apollo Palace (€€)

Quality hotel with many facilities, including swimming pool, tennis, basketball and volleyball. Restaurant and bar.

✉ Behind resort ☎ 26610-75433/75035 🕐 Apr–Oct

Christina (€–€€)

Attractive beachside hotel with restaurant and well-equipped guest rooms.

✉ Beachside location ☎ 26610-55294; www.hotelchristina.gr 🕐 May–Oct

MORAÏTIKA
Delfinia (€€)

A long-established, classic resort hotel which has expanded into a trio of separate buildings and kept pace with modernization. A few minutes from the centre, it has pleasant rooms and gardens that run down to the beach. Children are well looked after.

✉ Near beach ☎ 26610-76320; www.delfiniahotels.gr 🕐 Apr–Oct

Miramare Beach (€€–€€€)

Luxury hotel in its own grounds, fronted by a narrow beach. Gardens lead down to a beachside bar. Tennis courts. Courtesy bus service to Corfu Town.

✉ Near the beachfront ☎ 26610-75224–6; www.miramarebeach.gr
🕐 May–Oct

PÉRAMA
Aelos Beach (€€)
Very large hotel above Pérama. Several minutes to beach and resort. In-house amenities include swimming pool, sun terrace and pool-side bar. Children's play area. Water sports organized at the beach. Pets allowed.

✉ Overlooks resort ☎ 26610-33132/6; www.aelosbeach.gr ◷ Apr–Oct

Alexandros (€€–€€€)
At the heart of the resort, a few minutes from the shingle beach. There is a swimming pool in quiet gardens with attendant taverna. Water sports and other activities organized.

✉ Mid resort ☎ 26610-36855/6 ◷ Apr–Oct

RESTAURANTS

ÁGIOS GEÓRGIOS (SOUTHWEST)
Kafesas (€€)
See page 63.

Restaurant Panorama (€€)
Friendly family staff serve up excellent Greek specialities, including the best *kleftiko* (baked lamb) you'll ever taste.

✉ At the coast, near the centre of the resort ☎ 26620-52352 ◷ Lunch and dinner

ÁGIOS GÓRDIS
Sea Breeze (€€)
See page 63.

ALONÁKI
Alonáki Bay Taverna (€)
One of the most attractive and popular west-coast tavernas. Homey, with tree-shaded views to the sea. Good Corfiot home cooking, with some Italian flavours, fresh fish and a very potent local wine.

✉ Just north of Lake Korissión, on a rough track ☎ 26610-75872/76118 ◷ Lunch and dinner

BENÍTSES
O Paxinos (€€)
See page 63.

GASTOÚRI
Bella Vista (€€)
This long-established and very popular eatery has a fine leafy
terrace from which there are superb views of the mainland and
Achilleion Palace. The keynote meat dishes are well prepared and
all ingredients are well sourced and fresh.

✉ Gastoúri ☎ 26610-56232 🕐 Easter–Oct lunch and dinner, Nov–Easter
Fri–Sat dinner, Sun lunch

KÁVOS
Puff the Magic Dragon (€–€€)
There are good helpings of well-prepared Chinese and Indian
food under the same roof at this cheerful restaurant at the heart
of Kávos.

✉ Kávos ☎ 26620-61146 🕐 Lunch and dinner

The Drunken Squid (€–€€)
Next to Puff The Magic Dragon (see above) and run by the
same team, this Tex-Mex eatery masquerades as a Wild West
fort, complete with a working drawbridge. Big steaks and
traditional Mexican dishes are the order of the day at this
restaurant.

✉ Kávos ☎ 26620-61192 🕐 Lunch and dinner

KINOPIASTES
Tripa Taverna (€€€)
Popular venue where famous past guests include François
Mitterand, Aristotle Onassis and Jane Fonda, though not
necessarily together. There's a set menu with delicious *mezes*
and Corfiot favourites. Music and Greek dancing add to the fun.
Reservations are advised.

✉ Village is just off the road from Corfu Town to Sinarádes
☎ 26610-56333 🕐 Dinner

VIRÓS
Stamatis (€–€€)
See page 59.

SHOPPING

GASTOÚRI
Distillery Vassilakis
Unmissable. You will be 'spirited' inside before you are half in or out of the Achilleion gates opposite. Vassilakis has a huge selection of wines, spirits and liqueurs, as well as numerous kumquat products.
✉ Opposite the Achilleion ☎ 26610-52440

ENTERTAINMENT

BENÍTSES
A range of music bars and clubs, all offering much the same in music and a fairly frantic atmosphere. The choice includes Alexanders, Cheers Bar, Casanova's and Alcoholics Anonymous and Valentino's.

KÁVOS
Clubs and bars by the bucketload are the main point of Kávos and there's plenty to choose from. Torrents of drink tend to blur judgement but some venues are better than others. Popular clubs are Rocky's (see below), Futures, Empire, 42nd Street, Atlantis, Mr Bean's, Checkers, Limelight and Venue.

Rocky's
This is one of the better Kávos clubs, with friendly staff and British DJs playing a great mix of the latest international sounds.
✉ Main Street, Kávos ☎ 6944-24600 🕓 Until early hours

Index

Acknowledgements

The Automobile Association wishes to thank the following photographers, companies and picture libraries for their assistance in the preparation of this book.

Abbreviations for the picture credits are as follows – (t) top; (b) bottom; (l) left; (r) right; (c) centre; (AA) AA World Travel Library

4l Corfu Town, AA/C Sawyer; **4c** Ferry, AA/C Sawyer; **4r** Kalami beach, AA/S Outram; **5l** Mount Pantokratoras, AA/C Sawyer; **5c** Afionas, AA/C Sawyer; **6/7** Corfu Town, AA/C Sawyer; **8/9** Sheep grazing, AA/C Sawyer; **10l** Fisherman, AA/C Sawyer; **10r** Corfu Town back streets, AA/C Sawyer; **10/11** Houses, Liapades, AA/C Sawyer; **11c** Agios Spiridon, Corfu Town, AA/C Sawyer; **11b** Greek Flag, AA/C Sawyer; **12bl** Black Olives, AA/C Sawyer; **13t** Greek Salad, AA/C Sawyer; **13b**, Market Stall, Octupus, AA/C Sawyer; **14/15** Bottles of alcohol, AA/C Sawyer; **14** Grapes, AA/C Sawyer; **15** Kumquat tree, AA/C Sawyer; **16/17t** View over Kaiser's Throne, AA/C Sawyer; **16/17b** Corfu Town New Port, AA/C Sawyer; **17t** Municipal Art Gallery, Corfu Town, AA/C Sawyer; **17b** Dassia Watersports, AA/C Sawyer; **18/19** Bar in Sidari, AA/C Sawyer; **18b** Palaiokastritsa, AA/C Sawyer; **19tl** Museum of Asiatic Art, AA/C Sawyer; **19tr** Local woman, AA/S Outram; **19b** Palaiokastritsa, AA/C Sawyer; **20/21** Ferry, AA/C Sawyer; **24** Festival, AA/M Trelawney; **26/27** Hydrofoil, AA/C Sawyer; **28** Bus Stop, AA/C Sawyer; **29** Myrtiotissa beach, AA/C Sawyer; **31** Postbox, AA/C Sawyer; **34/35** Kalami beach, AA/S Outram; **36/37** Achilleion Palace, AA/S Day; **37** Inside Achilleion Palace, AA/S Outram; **38** St Spiridon, AA/C Sawyer; **38/39** Agios Spiridon, AA/M Trelawney; **40** Ayia Kyriaki, Angelokastro, AA/C Sawyer; **41** Angelokastro, AA/C Sawyer; **42** Corfu Town, AA/C Sawyer; **42/43** Back streets, Old Corfu Town, AA/C Sawyer; **44/45** Kalami Beach, AA/C Sawyer; **45** Lawrence Durrell, AA/C Sawyer; **46** Vlacherne Convent, AA/C Sawyer; **46/47** Kanoni Peninsula, AA/C Sawyer; **48/49t** Lake Korission, AA/C Sawyer; **48/49b** Lake Korission, AA/C Sawyer; **50** Archaeological Museum, AA/C Sawyer; **51** Archaeological Museum, Mons Repos room, AA/C Sawyer; **52** Palaiokastritsa Monastery, AA/C Sawyer; **52/53** Palaiokastritsa, AA/C Sawyer; **53** Palaiokastritsa, AA/C Sawyer; **54** Mount Pantokratoras, AA/J A Tims; **54/55** Mount Pantokratoras, AA/C Sawyer; **55** Mount Pantokratoras, AA/C Sawyer; **56/57** Taverna, AA/C Sawyer; **58** Rex Restaurant, Corfu Town, AA/C Sawyer; **60/61** Benitses nightlife, AA/C Sawyer; **62** Local people, AA/C Sawyer; **65** Excursion Boat, AA/C Sawyer; **66/67** Church of the Virgin Kremasti, AA/C Sawyer; **68/69** Museum of Asiatic Art, AA/C Sawyer; **70/71** Aqualand, AA/C Sawyer; **72/73** Myrtiotissa, AA/C Sawyer; **75** Hotel, AA/C Sawyer; **76** Olive wood souviners, AA/C Sawyer; **78/79** Afionas, AA/J A Tims; **81** Corfu Town rooftops, AA/C Sawyer; AA/C Sawyer; **82/83** St Jason and Sosipater, Paleopolis, AA/C Sawyer; **84/85** British Cemetery, AA/C Sawyer; **86/87** Municipal Art Gallery, AA/C Sawyer; **87** Orthodox Cathedral, Panagia Spiliotissa, AA/J A Tims; **88** Mons Repos Palace, AA/C Sawyer; **88/89** Mons Repos Palace, AA/S Outram; **90** Byzantine Museum, AA/C Sawyer; **91** New Fortress, Corfu Town, AA/S Outram; **92** Tomb of Menekrates, AA/S Outram; **93** Maitland Rotunda, AA/C Sawyer; **94** Fisherman, AA/S Day; **94/95** Old Fortress and Church of St George, AA/C Sawyer; **96** Palaiopolis, AA/S Day; **97** Museum of Asiatic Art, AA/C Sawyer; **98/99** Old Port area, Corfu Town, AA/S Outram; **99** Agios Spiridon, AA/C Sawyer; **101** Paxos, AA/A Sattin; **102** Town Hall, Corfu Town, AA/M Trelawney; **102/103** Statue of Polylas, AA/S Day; **103** First National Bank of Greece, Corfu Town, AA/M Trelawney; **104** San Rocco Square, AA/S Day; **104/105** San Rocco Square, AA/S Day; **105** Platitera monastery, AA/S Outram; **106** The Liston, Corfu Town, AA/C Sawyer; **119** Agios Stefanos, AA/C Sawyer; **120** Almiros, AA/J A Tims; **120/121** Antinioti Lagoon, AA/C Sawyer; **122/123** Agios Stefanos, AA/C Sawyer; **123** Agni, AA/C Sawyer; **124/125** Dassia, AA/C Sawyer; **126/127** Cape Asprokavas, AA/S Day; **127** Ano Korakianou, AA/C Sawyer; **128** Avalaki, AA/C Sawyer; **128/129** Avalaki, AA/C Sawyer; **130/131** Dassia, AA/J A Tims; **132/133** Kassiopi, AA/C Sawyer; **134** Kontokali, AA/J A Tims; **134/135** Kouloura, AA/C Sawyer; **136** Perithia, AA/S Outram; **136/137** Perithia, AA/S Outram; **138/139** Sidari, AA/C Sawyer; **139** St Nicholas, Sidari, AA/S Outram; **140** Ipsos Bay, AA/J A Tims; **149** Pelekas, AA/J A Tims; **150** Afionas, AA/J A Tims; **150/151** Agios Georgios, AA/C Sawyer; **152/153** Arillas Beach, AA/J A Tims; **154** Diapontia Island boat trip, AA/C Sawyer; **154/155** Doukades, AA/C Sawyer; **156/157** Ermones, AA/S Day; **157** Aqualand, AA/C Sawyer; **158/159** Glyfada, AA/C Sawyer; **160** Kaiser's Throne, AA/S Outram; **161** Pelekas, AA/M Trelawney; **162** Peroulades, AA/S Outram; **167** Moraitika, AA/S Outram; **168/169** Windsurf boards, Photodisc; **170/171** Agios Mattheos, AA/S Day; **172** Benitses, AA/C Sawyer; **174/175** Gardiki, AA/S Outram; **176** Kavos, AA/C Sawyer; **177** Lefkimmi, AA/C Sawyer; **178/179** Messongi, AA/S Outram; **179** Moraitika, AA/S Outram; **180** Aelos beach, AA/M Trelawney; **181** Church of the Forty Saints, Perivoli, AA/S Outram; **182t** History and Folklore Museum, Sinarades, AA/S Outram; **182b** Folklore Museum, Sinarades, AA/S Outram

Every effort has been made to trace the copyright holders, and we apologise in advance for any accidental errors. We would be happy to apply the corrections in the following edition of this publication.

Dear Reader

Your comments, opinions and recommendations are very important to us. So please help us to improve our travel guides by taking a few minutes to complete this simple questionnaire.

You do not need a stamp (unless posted outside the UK). If you do not want to cut this page from your guide, then photocopy it or write your answers on a plain sheet of paper.

Send to: **The Editor, AA World Travel Guides,**
FREEPOST SCE 4598, Basingstoke RG21 4GY.

Your recommendations...
We always encourage readers' recommendations for restaurants, nightlife or shopping – if your recommendation is used in the next edition of the guide, we will send you a **FREE AA Guide** of your choice from this series. Please state below the establishment name, location and your reasons for recommending it.

_____
_____
_____
_____
_____

Please send me **AA Guide** _____

About this guide...
Which title did you buy?
　AA _____
Where did you buy it? _____
When? m m / y y
Why did you choose this guide? _____
_____
_____
_____

Did this guide meet your expectations?

Exceeded ☐　Met all ☐　Met most ☐　Fell below ☐

Were there any aspects of this guide that you particularly liked? _____
_____
_____
_____

continued on next page...

Is there anything we could have done better? _____

_____

_____

_____

About you...

Name (Mr/Mrs/Ms) _____

Address _____

_____

_____ Postcode

Daytime tel nos _____

Email _____

Please only give us your mobile phone number or email if you wish to hear from us about
other products and services from the AA and partners by text or mms, or email.

Which age group are you in?
Under 25 ☐   25–34 ☐   35–44 ☐   45–54 ☐   55–64 ☐   65+ ☐

How many trips do you make a year?
Less than one ☐   One ☐   Two ☐   Three or more ☐

Are you an AA member? Yes ☐   No ☐

About your trip...

When did you book? m m / y y   When did you travel? m m / y y

How long did you stay? _____

Was it for business or leisure? _____

Did you buy any other travel guides for your trip?

If yes, which ones? _____

_____

_____

Thank you for taking the time to complete this questionnaire. Please send it to us as soon as
possible, and remember, you do not need a stamp (unless posted outside the UK).

> **AA** Travel Insurance call 0800 072 4168 or visit www.theAA.com